Awaken THE PURE Heart

Awaken THE PURE Heart

TALLAL ALIE TURFE

Visiting Professor
Department of Religious Studies
University of Detroit Mercy

AWAKEN THE PURE HEART

iUniverse books may be ordered through booksellers or by contacting:

iUniverse
1663 Liberty Drive
Bloomington, IN 47403
www.iuniverse.com
1-800-Authors (1-800-288-4677)

ISBN: 978-1-5320-3605-7 (sc)
ISBN: 978-1-5320-3607-1 (hc)
ISBN: 978-1-5320-3606-4 (e)

Library of Congress Control Number: 2017916274

Print information available on the last page.

iUniverse rev. date: 12/21/2017

This book is a gift to my three granddaughters, Mariam, Wanda, and Olivia, who personify the essence of the pure heart (*qalbun saleem*). Their hearts are pure in conduct, honesty, and integrity. They know and feel what it means to be devout Muslims, for their hearts are pure toward God and their families. They know how much I love them and that I'll always be there for them. I will always share our moments together, like breaking fast together during the month of Ramadan, having discussions on Islam, and having fun during our shopping sprees. These memories are kept deep in my heart, forever treasures of my heart as their spark deeply touches my soul. I am truly blessed to be their grandpa.

Contents

About the Author

As an American born with no formal training in Islamic studies, Tallal Turfe taught himself the Arabic alphabet so he could read the Qur'an in its original language. English translations of the Qur'an aided his understanding of the Arabic verses. For more than a half century, he taught young people about the Islamic faith, which further strengthened his knowledge and understanding of the religion. He also spoke to adult groups and at interfaith institutions.

As the growing Muslim community needed more Islamic centers and teachers, Tallal became more involved in studying, writing, and lecturing about Islamic topics. Religious scholars recognized his knowledge of Islam, and they frequently invited him to give presentations on the topic. Some of these topics centered on the common ground between Sunnis and Shi'as, such as the Qur'an, hadiths (traditions), and the core fundamentals of Islam, as well as the respect for unity in diversity. In addition, he made presentations to the broader interfaith community.

Tallal's undergraduate studies mainly focused on the subjects of psychology and sociology, while graduate studies were in the area of marketing, management, and finance. His keen understanding of the human persona qualified him as a frequent speaker on the topic of emotional intelligence as it related to the spiritual heart and Islam.

Tallal has authored six other books on religion, some of which are in several languages: (1) *Patience in Islam: Sabr*; (2) *Unity in Islam: Reflections and Insights*; (3) *Energy in Islam: A Scientific Approach to Preserving Our*

Health and the Environment; (4) *Children of Abraham: United We Prevail, Divided We Fail*; (5) *Know and Follow the Straight Path: Finding Common Ground between Sunnis and Shi'as*; and (6) *Remember Me, and I Will Remember You: Dhikr—The Soul of Islam*.

Tallal has served on a number of boards and was chairman of the Greater Detroit Interfaith Round Table of the National Conference for Community and Justice, currently the Michigan Roundtable for Diversity and Inclusion. He was a member of former president Bill Clinton's Call to Action: One America race relations group. Dubai Television identified him as a prominent and influential Arab American.

In October 1995, Tallal was the first Muslim to be presented with the Knight of Charity award by the Vatican-based Pontifical Institute for Foreign Missions. He was inducted into the International Heritage Foundation Hall of Fame for his global humanitarian efforts. In August 2000, he was one of two hundred political and religious leaders from around the world who participated in the Millennium World Peace Summit at the United Nations in New York. He has given other presentations on Islam at the United Nations—for example, education and parenting for peace, global ethics, and public diplomacy.

Tallal and his wife, Neemat, have been married for more than fifty years, and they have five children and twelve grandchildren.

Acknowledgments

This book is dedicated to the Twelfth Infallible Imam, Mohammad al-Mahdi, and may he pardon me for any errors I may have made.

This book is also dedicated to my parents, Hajj Alie Turfe and Hajjah Hassaney Turfe, who were constant and steadfast in their Islamic faith and good deeds. They inspired me to learn about Islam and its message to humankind.

It is hoped that this book will inspire those who wish to obtain a greater understanding of Islam, both Muslims and non-Muslims. In addition, a major outcome of this book is to reflect on the importance of becoming more unified in our faith, as well as respecting the faith of others.

The eminent and renowned scholar Ayatollah Imam Abdul Latif Berry, founder of the Islamic Institute of Knowledge, spurred me to enhance my knowledge of Islam and write books on the subject. I am very grateful to him for opening my mind to the many facets of the religion and for nurturing me to explore the depths of its philosophy. He always urged me to undertake a study of the contemporary facets of Islam, thereby enlightening Muslims and non-Muslims in America and abroad.

Pure Heart: A Poem
Tallal Alie Turfe

Awaken O' pure heart!
Refresh and pray to start.
Seeking the Lord's embrace.
Blessing it with His Grace.
And spark the light inside
So that it may abide.
Awake to a new start.
As angels guard the heart.

Introduction

In America, we live in a fast-paced, self-indulgent society of pleasure-seeking people, predicating their lifestyles on consumer-oriented and materialistic notions. Influenced by the world around them, their hearts may become faithless, dishonest, deceptive, distressed, and, at times, evil. Hence, their hearts become damaged. However, in the quiet of their solitude, they can deeply reflect on how to become devout and pious as they awaken the pure heart.

The Damaged Heart

For those who deliberately abandon true guidance, God will send them the jinn (evil one) to lead them astray and show them the path to hell. The evil one is Satan. Abu'l-Faraj ibn al-Jawzi of the twelfth century describes how the devil enters into the heart and corrupts it:

> The heart is like a fort that is surrounded by a wall and the wall has gates from which it can be torn down. In it lays the mind. The angels frequent that fort and next to that fort are places where the desires lie. And the devils enter into this surrounding area without being prevented from doing so. And the war exists between the inhabitants of the fort and the inhabitants of the surrounding areas.

The devils never stop circling the fort and looking for an opening where the guard is heedless and from where he can tear down the fort. It is obligatory for the guards to be completely aware of all of the gates of the fort that must be guarded as well as all of its weak points from which destruction can come. The guard cannot take a break because the enemy never takes a break.

The fort is lit by the remembrance of God and faith in Him. In it is a polished looking glass through which (the guardians) can then see anything that passes by. The first thing that Satan does is to blow smoke into the fort to make its wall black. This causes rust and damage in the fort. Sound thought repels Satan and remembrance of God cleans the looking glass.

The enemy has carriages and sometimes they are able to enter the fort. The guards may come upon them and force them to leave. Perhaps they may enter due to the heedlessness or carelessness of the guards. Perhaps, due to the smoke and the rust, Satan enters through any way and he is not perceived. Perhaps the guard is injured by the heedlessness or is taken prisoner and led to the following of the desires. (Al-Ashqar 2005)

The Gift of Solitude

How can we slow down in the fast-paced society in which we live? How can we escape from the social media that doesn't leave much time for ourselves? Can we truly find time to avoid the hustle and bustle of our daily activities, which doesn't allow us much downtime for just being alone with ourselves? Rather than being connected to our smartphones and social media, we need to find downtime to reflect in solitude so as to contemplate on important activities such as prayer, supplication, and charitable causes. In a nutshell, we need to find time to be alone and think of those things that enhance our spiritual well-being.

According to a report by Common Sense Media, the total time teens and tweens in America spend watching television and movies, playing video games, reading, listening to music, and checking social media is about nine hours daily. Importantly, this does not include time spent using media at school or for their homework (Wallace 2015). Time management is a concern for how we conduct our daily activities. It is the process of planning and exercising conscious control over the amount of time spent on specific activities, including prayer. However, the combined total time of the five daily prayers only takes about one half hour to perform, which includes the ablution (Turfe 2016).

Loneliness is inner emptiness. Solitude is inner fulfillment. Solitude is more a state of mind and heart than it is a place (Foster 2017). Each of us has moments when we need to refocus and reconnect. Solitude affords us the opportunity to do just that. Wherever we may be, we can take time out to enjoy solitude, for it is an inner posture of the heart. Our self-awareness and self-consciousness are heightened as we start spending more time in meditation, conversing with our inner selves, discussing various decisions and choices within ourselves, and seeing that small things do matter.

In seeking out more ways to connect with others, rarely do we take the time to sit down and think about ourselves introspectively. We live in a world where privacy and solitude have become a scarce commodity yet are invaluable for creativity and for finding inner peace (Fullerton 2010). We are bombarded by social media that takes away valuable time for us to be alone in our solitude. Solitude is an invaluable method for contemplation and reflection. It provides Muslims with a gateway to our five daily prayers to make them more actionable and meaningful. It also reduces stress so we can better concentrate on our prayer and not hurry through it.

Henry David Thoreau remarked that even though his closest neighbor was only a mile away, so great was his feeling of solitude. It is not that he gave up society but that he exchanged the insignificant society of humans for the superior society of nature. What Thoreau meant by solitude is not loneliness or isolation but self-communion and introspection. Solitude means that he was on his own spiritually, confronting the full array of nature's bounty without any intermediaries. Hence, the importance of worldly affairs faded away (Thoreau 2013). When we spend a day at the beach facing the ocean and completely closed off from other people, we stand alone in solitude. At that moment, we watch the oncoming waves with a great deal of intensity and concentration as the rays of the sun beam across the water. For us, solitude at that moment is a way we connect to the vastness and beauty of God's creation.

While in solitude, we can focus on what is rousing in our hearts in preparation of our daily activities, brief escape from society, or readiness for prayer. In silence and solitude, we can free ourselves of distractions and overcome resistance from others. We need to free our minds in order to spiritually connect to God, seeking His blessing and mercy. Therefore, in solitude a transformation in the heart results in seeking God, rather than just seeking from God; in serving God, rather than just worshipping God; and in remembering God, rather than just reminders about God. Solitude is vital to maintaining and sustaining a pure heart (*qalbun saleem*). Moreover, children should also learn to enjoy solitude. True, children need to fill their minds with information derived from life's experiences as part of the learning process. However, they also need time to process that information and to develop their own spiritual thoughts, experiencing worship without distraction as they, too, become comfortable with solitude. Truly, solitude is a gift from God.

Awaken the Pure Heart

All alone in the wilderness surrounded by ferocious beasts of prey and dead carcasses, he is fearful of the fate that awaits him. Having abandoned his family and faith, he now stands isolated in the loneliness of the vast desert, helpless in the darkness of despair. It has been months since he was in touch with civilization, absorbed by the fast pace of the hustle and bustle on the crowded streets of the Big Apple. He had it all—money, luxurious cars, and the life of ease. Yet somewhere along the way, he thought he was on top of the world, impregnated and immersed in the love of life, not in need of anyone but himself.

This is a case of one who forgot God and didn't pray or fast during the month of Ramadan. In short, he dwelled in complacency, thinking his wealth was his best companion, a wealth that controlled and consumed him. Wandering through the wilderness was not a journey but a drifting away from the straight path in an endless web of desolation. When he was absorbed by the materialistic fangs of worldly endeavors, he was deluded in thinking he had no difficulties. His path was not that of spiritual enlightenment but rather a sinful disposition that firmly implanted its dastardly sting within the depths of his heart. The darkness of soul and betrayal of heart were his companions, as he was lost and could not find his way back to the righteous path of piety. But now in the depths of his conscience, a voice awakens his soul and stimulates his inner heart. With no food, no water, the taste of death is imminent. He cries out, "Dear God! Help me!"

Unlike this lost soul, as we progress on the path of awakening, we overcome the ego and let the purity of our hearts guide us through difficult times. As we let go of the ego's need to have more, the energy within our contented hearts will find the straight path and lead us out of the wilderness. What is needed is an enlightened awakening of consciousness to lead us out of the darkness of evil. Evil cannot stand to be seen because once it is made conscious, it loses its power and can no longer act itself out through us. Hence, we will be on the road of recovery to strengthening and purifying our hearts. The contented heart allows us to regain the serenity of our souls. The pure heart allows us to reach the realization that everything we need to progress spiritually is within us.

As for the lost soul in the wilderness, his heart accumulated many scars because of his neglect to find the spiritual spark within his heart. Healing of the heart begins when we feel the connection of God within us. Before we can awaken the heart, we need to heal it by letting go of the negative energies and thoughts to which we have been attached. We must remember God, ask for His forgiveness, and be grateful to Him for everything He has given us. The more we acknowledge His blessings the more our hearts will open to receive His infinite mercy and kindness.

Our hearts awaken when we begin to be aware of it, as we embrace the divine presence of God.

Faith is not just agreement and obedience with certain facts and certain rules but rather a person's dedication to God's will and the recognition of His sovereignty. Occasionally, people may lose faith, if what they hoped for didn't come about. In distressed times, they tend to move away from being optimistic to being pessimistic. While life is beset with many problems, faith steers us in the direction of things getting better. Faith is the tool that helps replenish abundance in the heart and soul, not just in the mind. Faith is at the core of the heart. Faith may lie dormant until awakened by the pure and contented heart.

The heart is a muscular organ about the size of a fist, located just behind and slightly left of the breastbone. The heart pumps blood through the network of arteries and veins called the cardiovascular system (Hoffman 2014). In addition, the heart is the spiritual control center of life, the very center of our existence. Hence, the heart is the very essence of who we are. The heart is the center of the soul. It is the seat of our emotional intelligence, intention, and desires. It is the point of our personal contact with God, as He judges us according to what is in our hearts.

In Islam, believers are those who completely submit their wills to the will of God by firmly establishing faith in their hearts. In this regard, including various descriptions and connotations, the heart is mentioned at least 130 times in the Qur'an. While physicians restrict the heart's function to pumping blood throughout the human body, the Qur'an refers to the heart as an organ that is the center of reasoning, intentions, and decision-making. Hence, these descriptions of the heart address the physical, mental, emotional, and spiritual aspects of the human persona.

Scientists have recently proven that the heart is as conscious as the human brain and has its own form of intelligence that accepts, comprehends, and stores knowledge. Furthermore, scientists also believe that the heart communicates with both the brain and the rest of the human body through the nervous system, pulse waves, certain hormones, and energetic waves. The heart's electromagnetic field envelops every cell in the human body (El-Naggar).

The heart is more than the most important organ in the human body. It is also the quintessence of our spiritual and emotional well-being. Whether experiencing acceptance or rejection, our hearts are aroused. Acceptance causes the heart to be elated or jubilant, while rejection causes the heart to be saddened or troubled. In addition, empathy is a trait of a compassionate heart, while hatred is a trait of a troubled heart.

While the intellect of the brain renders decisions as to how opposing parties can resolve conflicts, the intellect of the heart will bring about a happier win/win situation for both sides of these conflicts. Toward this end, the brain and heart work in concert with each other to resolve problems and troubled waters. While the brain can solve deep-rooted medical problems, such as cancer via scientific methods, it may fail because it is not in touch with our deeper feelings that generate from the heart.

A cancer patient may be cured of the disease, but the process of the mind is cluttered with many theories and experiments as to how to proceed, thereby causing the patient undue stress along the way. As a result, the mind is pushed in many directions with all kinds of data, some of which are useless, thereby making the patient more fearful of his or her condition than he or she was before medical tests and medication were administered. Perhaps the patient wasn't yet ready to undergo numerous tests because he or she was emotionally and physically worn out. Furthermore, treatment was not in touch with the deeper feelings of the heart. The heart goes a long way in preparing the patient to endure aggressive tests and treatments. As the heart showers the patient with serenity and ease, the difficulties and worries slowly dissipate, and pain begins to subside. Hence, awakening the heart makes the brain more thoughtful, attentive, invigorated, perceptive, and purified. It is the heart that is with truth and pure intention.

The heart conditions our overall sense of well-being, and it is not possessed with itself, as the brain tends to be. As the seat of our feelings, the heart is a navigational system that renders intensified mental clarity and intuition. These feelings can result in broken hearts, such as happened to the main character, Heathcliff, in Emily Bronte's book, *Wuthering Heights*:

"You love me—then what right had you to leave me? ...
You, of your own will, did it. I have not broken your
heart—you have broken it; and in breaking it, you have
broken mine."

We often hear that someone has died from a broken heart. That is
because we associate our feelings with our hearts. Is there a connection
between the heart and mind that they work together? The brain controls
the central nervous system that is connected to our hearts. However,
what is good for the heart is good for the brain, and what is bad for
the heart is bad for the brain. In effect, both the heart and brain work
together.

According to the American Heart Association, the 2017 data reveal
that heart disease remains as the number-one cause of death in the
United States. About 2,200 Americans die of cardiovascular disease
each day, an average of one death every forty seconds. Coronary heart
disease is the leading cause (45.1 percent) of deaths attributable to
cardiovascular disease, followed by stroke (16.5 percent), high blood
pressure (9.1 percent), heart failure (8.5 percent), diseases of the arteries
(3.2 percent), and other cardiovascular diseases.

About 610,000 people die of heart disease in the United States every
year—that's one in every four deaths (CDC 2015). About 47 percent of
sudden cardiac deaths occur outside a hospital, which suggests that many
people with heart disease don't act on early warning signs (CDC 2002).

What, then, is causing such massive heart disease? Could it be that
we are dying from broken hearts? And if so, what is causing them to
break? It seems that high levels of stress interfere with the electrical
rhythm of the heart. Could it be that our loss of connection to the natural
world, created by modern life, is the original wound, and this primary
separation is causing our hearts to break? (Montgomery 2008).

Both the heart and the brain must work in unison to sustain life in
the human body. The heart beats around one hundred thousand times
daily, thirty-five million times a year. During one's lifetime, the brain
and heart work together to engineer three billion heartbeats. However,
the heart can also beat by itself without the assistance of the brain; it's

called automaticity. Even if the heart is disconnected from working with the brain, it will continue to beat at a set rate. It's called the intrinsic heart rate, usually around 90–110 beats per minute. If one has a heart transplant, and the heart is transplanted into another human, it's not connected with the brain. But that heart continues to beat at a set intrinsic rate. In addition to the intrinsic heartbeat that the heart has all by itself, the automatic nervous system is a separate part of the brain and brain function that can neither speed up nor slow down the heart. With that regulation, the heart rate then has a great deal of variability throughout the day, depending on what the body needs (Eckhardt).

Awaken the Pure Heart illustrates the importance of the heart in our daily activities, not only in the physical sense but the mental, emotional, and spiritual aspects as well. We will explore how emotional intelligence has an impact on the pure heart from the vantage point of whether or not the heart can actually think. In addition, the characteristics, categories, and spiritual cures for the diseases of the heart will be discussed. Furthermore, the importance of the Qur'an as a healing source for the distressed pure heart will be emphasized.

Chapter 1

Emotional Intelligence

A relatively recent concept, emotional intelligence, has emerged that sheds light on how the heart is able to think as well as feel. Toward this end, several questions need to be addressed. What is emotional intelligence, and how did it evolve? How does emotional intelligence impact our daily lives as Muslims? What is the relationship between emotional intelligence, the intellect, and the heart?

Historical Development of Emotional Intelligence

Many intelligence quotient (IQ) scholars held the notion that intelligence is inherited and cannot be changed. They endorsed widely different estimates of the heritability of intelligence, ranging from 40 percent to 80 percent (Rosenfeld 1977). IQ is a total score derived from several standardized tests designed to assess human intelligence. In 1985, Reuven Bar-On, a clinical psychologist, coined the term emotional quotient (or EQ) (Bar-On 1996). Later, other researchers, such as Peter Salovey and John Mayer, modeled the term emotional intelligence (EI)

(Salovey 2004). Thereafter, Daniel Goleman popularized EI in his book of the same name (Goleman 1995).

Emotional intelligence recognizes, understands, and manages our own emotions. It also recognizes, understands, and influences the emotions of others. According to Goleman, life's successes are largely the result of how we manage our emotions rather than of our intellectual aptitudes. In addition, why we lack success in life may be due to mismanagement of our emotions. His research explains why people with modest IQs may perform better in life's experiences than those with high IQs. Furthermore, emotional intelligence, unlike IQ, can be developed and improved throughout life.

Impact of Emotional Intelligence on Our Daily Lives as Muslims

Developing emotional intelligence skills allows people to think more clearly under pressure, eliminating time wasted by feelings of anger, anxiety, and fear. People with high emotional intelligence skills get along better and don't let anxieties and frustrations get in the way of efficiently solving problems. It increases the understanding between people, which minimizes time wasted arguing and being defensive. How this emotional intelligence unfolds is what Goleman describes as personal competence and social competence:

Personal Competence

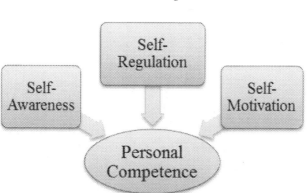

Social Competence

Self-awareness, self-regulation, and self-motivation are intrapersonal (i.e., within the individual), while empathy and managing relationships are interpersonal (between people). We must have good intrapersonal skills to develop good interpersonal skills. Intrapersonal skills derive from the ability to be aware of, make sense of, use, and manage the information from our own emotional states; for example, assertiveness, self-regard, and independence. Interpersonal skills derive from the ability to perceive the moods, motivations, and intentions of others; for example, social responsibility.

Self-awareness means having a profound understanding of our emotions and how our feelings affect ourselves and other people. Self-awareness is having an accurate understanding of how we interact and behave with each other, how sensitive we are to the emotional well-being of others, and how we are able to convey this awareness to others. It is recognizing when we become negative, angry, or defensive. Self-awareness is recognizing our feelings as they occur, with a confident sense of integrity and openness and with a high level of self-esteem. The Qur'an reminds us of the importance of knowing ourselves and knowing our Creator:

The Prophet said, "Such a person as recites the Qur'an and masters it by heart, will be with the (angels) honorable and obedient (in heaven). And such a person as exerts himself to learn the Qur'an by heart, and recites it with great difficulty, will have a double reward." (*Sahih Bukhari*, vol. 6, book 65, chapter 1, Hadith 4937)

The Qur'an also encourages Muslims to become aware of themselves, knowledgeable about their emotions, and to completely recognize their feelings. Furthermore, the Qur'an emphasizes that change begins from within us:

> And be not like unto those who forsook God! So He made them forsake their own selves; these are the transgressors. (Qur'an 59:19)

> And (*also*) in your own selves; will you not then see? (Qur'an 51:21)

> Verily, God changes not the condition of a people until they change what is in themselves. (Qur'an 13:11)

Prophet Muhammad had said, "Whoever knows himself will then know his Lord" (*Bihar al-Anwar*, Al-Allamah Al-Majlisi, vol. 2, p. 32; and *Tafseer Al-Razi*, Al-Fakir Al-Razi, vol. 1, p. 91). According to Sayed Moustafa al-Qazwini, recognizing our own self-worth prevents us from being misguided. As such, the basis of true humility derives from knowing our own self-worth and being willing to submit to God (Al-Qazwini 2011).

Relative to self-awareness or self-cognition, Imam Ali ibn Abi Talib said, "O' my God! You know me better than myself, and I know myself more than they know. O' my God! Make us better than what they think and forgive us what they do not know" (*Nahjul Balagha*, Saying 100). Imam Ali expressed the purest thing that is acquired by anyone, which is that he recognized himself through his heart nourished by God. As such, Imam Ali's self-awareness was that he knew God by the light that manifested and resided in his heart.

Through self-regulation, we are able to promote an atmosphere of trust and fairness. Time management is regulated by not engaging in negativism and redundancy. With self-regulation, we can rid ourselves of anxiety and despair by maintaining an emotional perspective. We can relax in pressure situations and handle feelings and information in such a way that they are properly managed. By grasping the beliefs and values that lie behind our feelings, we can find productive ways to handle our anxiety, despair, and fear. Self-regulation also requires us to be moderate in spending our own well-earned wealth and avoiding waste:

> And those who, when they spend, are neither extravagant nor niggardly but are stationed between the two (*extremes*). (Qur'an 25:67)

> "O' Children of Adam! Be you adorned at every time of prostration and eat you and drink you and commit you not excesses; verily, He (*God*) loves not the extravagant." (Qur'an 7:31)

Bringing the Muslim leadership together requires a great deal of self-motivation, and the leadership must be passionate about achieving the unity. Highly motivated people are driven by their desire to achieve, rather than driven by external rewards. They do not admit defeat, as they are determined to achieve the goal of unity. They are able to channel emotions to achieve a goal, and they persevere in the face of frustration, undaunted by external pressure. They are able to regroup quickly after a setback. Muslims should perpetuate in their endeavors to do good deeds in order to be rewarded by God and to gain God's pleasure. For example, attending funerals and visiting the sick pleases God. God rewards all of these actions because they bring joy to the hearts of the believers. We should seek God's guidance in building our self-motivation and self-confidence. We should remain in a positive state of mind, whatever the circumstances. It is wrong for people to lack self-motivation and self-confidence because of errors they have committed:

"O' my Lord! Expand for me my breast, and make easy for me my task, and loosen the knot of my tongue, that they may understand my speech." (Qur'an 20:25–28)

And lose you not heart and grieve you not, for you shall gain the upper hand, if you (*only*) be (*true*) believers. (Qur'an 3:139)

The prophets and messengers of God were men who lived the life of the pure heart. God chooses only those who are pure in heart to deliver His message:

Prophet Muhammad said, "God has not sent any prophet or apostle unless he has completed his intellect and his intellect is superior to the intellect of his entire nation." (Al-Kafi, vol. 1, p. 13)

Imam Hassan al-Askari, the Eleventh Imam, said, "Verily, God found the heart of Muhammad the best and with the greatest capacity so He chose him for prophethood." (Bihar al-Anwar, vol. 18, p. 205)

Another example is the connectivity of the pure heart of Prophet Muhammad with that of Imam Ali ibn Abi Talib:

Have We not expanded (*for*) you your breast? And removed from you your burden that weighed down your back? (Qur'an 94:1–3)

These verses clearly demonstrate that the heart of Prophet Muhammad was purified and that his union with another pure heart, Imam Ali ibn Abi Talib, removed his burden. Even the marriage of Imam Ali with Fatima, daughter of Prophet Muhammad, was a union of two pure hearts, and this purity extended to their children, Imam Hassan and Imam Hussein:

> And God only wishes to remove all abomination from
> you, you Members of the Family, and to make you pure
> and spotless. (Qur'an 33:33)

In order to win the pleasure of God, we should try to follow the example of these role models by purifying our hearts. Some other attributes that win the pleasure of God are (a) *sadaqah*, or giving of charity; (b) *ma'roof*, or courtesy that includes all forms of righteous action, particularly when helping others; and (c) *sulha*, or reconciliation that brings Muslims in dispute back to Islam to resolve their differences.

Empathy is the ability to exchange information on a meaningful level. With empathy, people become proficient in skills essential for organizing groups and building teams, negotiating solutions, reconciling conflict among others, developing consensus, and creating personal connections. Empathy is being compassionate to the feelings and concerns of others as well as respecting their viewpoints. It is about saving the lives of others and also about sharing the happiness as well as the pain of others:

> He who slays any one (man), without (*that being for*)
> murder, or for mischief in the land, (*it shall be*) as though
> he has slain mankind as a whole; and he who saves it (*a
> human life*), shall be as though he has saved mankind as
> a whole." (Qur'an 5:32)

> What would make thee know the path that is steep?
> (*It is*) the freeing a slave or a captive, or feeding in the
> day of hunger, to an orphan, being near of kin, or to the
> poor one lying in the dust. Besides this, to be of those
> who believe, and enjoin steadfastness on each other, and
> enjoin mercy on each other. (Qur'an 90:12–17)

With managing relationships, people are more productive, as they do not squander time arguing and second-guessing themselves. They are aware of the emotions and feelings of others, and they are good listeners. They are able to collaborate with others in order to bring about a solution. They recognize when others are distressed, and they manage emotions with social competence and skill. Managing relationships is vital in a marriage because the love between husband and wife is the grace of God. Managing relationships between others, especially maintaining bonds of kinship with relatives (*silat ur-rahim*), enjoys extraordinary importance in Islam:

> And of His signs is that He created for you from yourselves, mates that you may dwell (*inclined*) unto them, and caused between you love and compassion. (Qur'an 30:21)

> O you who believe! Be always upright for God, bearing witness with justice, and let not hatred of a people incite you not to act equitably; act you equitably that is nearer to piety. (Qur'an 5:8)

> Then belike you are, if you hold authority, that you make mischief in the earth and sever the ties of kinship! Those are they whom had cursed God, and so had He made them deaf and blinded their eyes. (Qur'an 47:22–23)

Let's just reflect on one of the aspects of emotional intelligence: team capabilities or team building. Team building is a social-competence skill, and the coalition unity can support, delineate, and attain success through collaborative goal setting and utilizing its capacity to achieve them. Critical issues are defined and discussed. Team building provides a vehicle for winning the unity as the participants comprehend and grasp the know-how needed to be major contributors. Team-building members will acquire the knowledge, skills, and abilities to

+ define what is expected from the coalition unity and the expectations of its stakeholders as to goals and outcome;
+ develop rules of engagement for the team members;

+ identify barriers and critical success factors that enable the team to complete its mission;
+ define critical team responsibilities and accountabilities as well as measurements of progress and success; and
+ develop problem-solving and problem-prevention techniques as well as feedback.

Leaders and team builders will experience various functions of emotional intelligence:

+ feelings
+ bodily arousal
+ sense of purpose
+ socially expressive

Functions of Emotional Intelligence

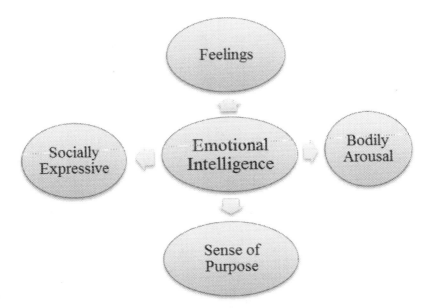

The primary aspect of emotional intelligence for Muslim leaders is to create good feelings in the people they lead. They do this by maintaining those same positive feelings in themselves. In addition, they have to create change, sustain change, and build an emotional intelligence component within themselves. Emotions are subjective feelings (i.e., they make us feel in a particular way). Our bodies are prepared for action and are activated in coping behavior during emotion. In life, we have a sense of purpose in that we give emotion its goal-directed force and become motivated to take action and to cope with emotion-causing circumstances. Becoming socially expressive includes our postures, gestures, vocalizations, and facial expressions that make our emotions public. It also includes our verbal and nonverbal communication, as well as how to interpret a situation and how to react to that situation.

Most effective leaders are value driven, flexible, informal, open, and frank. They are more connected to people and to networks. More especially, they exude resonance. They have genuine passion for their missions, and that passion is contagious. Their enthusiasm and excitement spread spontaneously, invigorating those who lead. The stronger a person is in emotional intelligence, the better leader he or she will become. Unless we are aware of our own emotions, we will not know how to control them.

Understanding emotional intelligence can be very effective in winning the unity among Muslims. If we are to succeed in this endeavor, then we must be able to control our emotions and be empathetic toward others. We must be ready to submit our will to the will of God, as we proceed toward a more unified Muslim society. We pray to God to continue to guide us in our quest for unity and a more peaceful and prosperous life.

Relationship of the Heart to the Emotional System and Brain

While research has underscored the importance of emotional intelligence to the heart, what is the importance of the heart to the function of our physical, mental, spiritual, and emotional system? How do the heart and brain interconnect? A cursory look at the scientific studies on the importance of the heart follows:

Priority of the deeds of the heart is more important than the deeds of the limbs and senses (Baianonie 1997). Awareness begins in the heart, not the brain (Bechara 2004). According to a 2004 article in the *Journal of Alternative and Complementary Medicine*, Dr. Rollin McCraty, from the HeartMath Institute, concludes that the heart seems to know the emotional future. It is able to emotionally sense events and react before they actually happen. The heart senses intuitively and then conveys this information to the brain to prepare for a response. In other words, the heart responds up to six seconds before the brain does. The heart sends input to the brain, not vice versa, which goes against the standard biological model that the brain is the command center of the body (Walton 2015).

The heart is an information-processing center that can learn, remember, and act independently of the cranial brain and actually can connect and send signals to key brain areas, such as the amygdala, thalamus, and hypothalamus, which regulate perceptions and emotions (Surel 2015). Research studies have detected in individuals up to five feet apart that the heart's electromagnetism can affect and even synchronize with another participant's brain waves (i.e., the brain seems to be innately sensitive and receptive to the heart "energy" of others) (McCraty December 2004–February 2005). The heart actually sends more signals to the brain than the brain sends to the heart (Surel 2015).

The concept of emotional intelligence and results from scientific research on the spirituality of the heart are in consonance with the teachings of Islam, which teaches us to control our emotions in order to purify our hearts. Moreover, in Islam the faculty of consciousness that is related to the intellect is the heart, which experiences all emotions. The question remains as to whether the heart can think.

Chapter 2

Can the Heart Think?

Several verses in the Qur'an disclose that the heart does, in fact, have the capability to think, store thoughts, feel, and interact with the brain in controlling the thinking process:

> And of them are those who hearken unto thee, and We have cast veils over their hearts lest they understand it, and a heaviness into their ears; and (*even*) if they see every sign they will not believe in it; to the extent that when they come to thee they only dispute with thee, those who disbelieve say: "This is naught but the legends of the ancients." (Qur'an 6:25)

> Verily We have caused veils over their hearts lest they understand it and in their ears a heaviness; and if thou calls them unto guidance, never will they in that case get guided aright at all. (Qur'an 18:57)

> What! Have not they travelled in the earth that they should have hearts to understand them with, or ears

to hear them with? For verily blind are not the eyes but blind are the hearts that are in the breasts. (Qur'an 22:46)

The term *understanding* in each of the three verses above denotes seeing. While our ears hear things and our eyes look at things, it is understanding that determines the meaning of what we are hearing or looking at. We can hear something with our ears, and we can look at something with our eyes, but only with understanding can we know the meaning of what we are hearing or looking at. Hence, what we are looking at is actually seeing it.

Previously, we have been led to believe that scientists only focused on the heart's responses to the brain's commands. Now, scientific research has disclosed that communication between the heart and brain is dynamic and ongoing. Each organ, the heart or the brain, engages in a two-way dialogue, constantly influencing each other.

Scientists in the field of neurocardiology have discovered that the heart possesses its own intrinsic nervous system—a network of nerves so functionally sophisticated as to earn the description of a "heart brain." (McCraty December 2004–February 2005). Neurophysiologists discovered a neural pathway and mechanism whereby input from the heart to the brain could inhibit or facilitate the brain's electrical activity (McCraty 2002). The heart's intrinsic nervous system operates and processes information independently of the brain or nervous system, which allows a heart transplant to work (Murphy et al 2000). The heart communicates information to the brain and throughout the body via electromagnetic field interactions, and the heart's magnetic component is about five hundred times stronger than the brain's magnetic field (McCraty, Bradley, and Tomasino 2004).

Dr. J. Andrew Armour, a researcher and specialist in neurocardiology at the Hopital du Sacre-Coeur, University of Montreal, is also a member of the Scientific Advisory Board at HeartMath Institute. Dr. Armour first introduced the term *heart brain* in 1991. According to Dr. Armour, the heart's complex intrinsic nervous system qualified as a "little brain." Dr. Armour discovered the heart contains a cell type known as intrinsic cardiac adrenergic (ICA), which synthesizes and releases neurotransmitters once thought to be produced only by neurons in the brain and nerve ganglia.

Since 1991, the HeartMath Institute, located in Boulder Creek, California, has researched and developed reliable scientifically based tools to help people bridge the connection between their hearts and minds and deepen their connection with the hearts of others. Dr. Armour says that the heart brain is an "intricate network of several types of neurons, neurotransmitters, proteins, and support cells, like those found in the brain proper. Research has shown that the heart communicates into the brain in four major ways: neurologically (through the transmission of nerve impulses), biochemically (via hormones and neurotransmitters), biophysically (through pressure waves), and energetically (through electromagnetic field interactions)." Its elaborate circuitry enables it to act independently of the cranial brain—to learn, remember, and even feel and sense (Childre 2013).

Continued research has made great strides in understanding the many functions of the heart, some of which are listed below (McCraty 2015):

1. The heart sends emotional and intuitive signals as it processes and decodes intuitive information.
2. The heart directs and aligns many systems in the body so that they can function in harmony with one another.
3. The heart is in constant communication with the brain, and both the heart and brain receive and respond to information about a future event before the event actually happens.
4. The heart's intrinsic brain and nervous system relay information back to the brain in the cranium, creating a two-way communication system between heart and brain:

Emotional Intelligence Flows from Heart to Brain

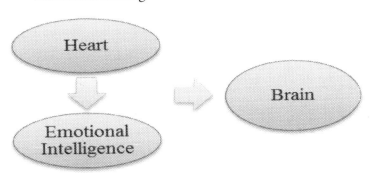

5. The heart makes many of its own decisions.
6. The heart starts beating in the unborn fetus before the brain has been formed, a process scientists call autorhythmic.
7. Humans form an emotional brain long before a rational one and a beating heart before either.
8. The heart has its own independent complex nervous system known as "the brain of the heart."

Emotional Intelligence versus IQ

International search firm Egon Zehnder International analyzed 515 senior executives and discovered that those who were strongest in emotional intelligence were more likely to succeed than those strongest in either IQ (intelligence quotient) or relevant previous experience. The Carnegie Institute of Technology carried out research that showed that 85 percent of our financial success is due to skills in "human engineering," personality, and ability to communicate, negotiate, and lead. They found that only 15 percent is due to technical ability. In other words, people skills or skills highly related to emotional intelligence are crucial skills (Deutschendorf 2015).

According to Dr. Daniel Goleman, people's emotional intelligence enables them to succeed in life as much as or more than their IQ (intelligence quotient). Through vivid examples, Dr. Goleman delineates five crucial skills of emotional intelligence and shows how they determine our success in relationships, work, and even our physical well-being. Dr. Goleman argues that our IQ view of intelligence is far too narrow. Instead, he makes the case for emotional intelligence being the strongest indicator of human success. He defines emotional intelligence in terms of self-awareness, altruism, personal motivation, empathy, and the ability to love and be loved by friends, partners, and family members (Goleman 2005). Truly, emotional intelligence of the heart is the doorway to spiritual intelligence, which is our connection with God. The heart is the electrical powerhouse of the human body. Each heartbeat begins with a pulse of electricity through the heart muscle. Following are facts about how the heart functions:

Heart Facts

✦	Heart begins to form in the fetus before the brain.
✦	Average heart beats 110,000 times a day, 40 million times a year.
✦	Heart produces enough power in 1 hour to lift 2,000 pounds 3 feet off the ground.
✦	Source of the heartbeat is in the heart, not the brain.
✦	After heart transplant, heart and brain do not reconnect; heart beats on its own.
✦	Electrical impulse of each heartbeat can be measured 3 to 4 feet from the body.
✦	Electrical impulse of the heart is 40 to 60 times stronger than the brain.
✦	Heart sends more information to the brain than the brain does to the heart.
✦	Heart's vascular system is 60,000 miles long; can wrap around the earth twice.

Source: Courtesy of HeartMath LLC

Source of Intelligence

From the above research and findings, the question arises as to whether intelligence is in the brain or the heart. Aristotle was of the view that the heart is the organ of intelligence (Frampton 1991).

Interconnect of Intellect with Brain and Heart

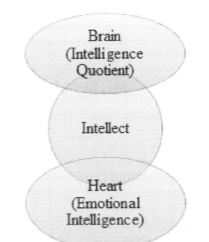

Aristotle noticed that the body grows cold when the heart stops beating, which led him to assume that the heart produces the body's heat. To protect the heart from overheating, Aristotle assigned the function of cooling the unremitting heart to the brain. Furthermore, by Aristotle's time it was known that human voice is supplied by air exhaled from the lungs. Hence, he reasoned that the heart supplies words, and they come out together with the voice as they roll out of the chest cavity (Ghilan 2012). The interconnect of intellect with the brain and heart, as believed by Aristotle, was further hypothesized in the Arab world and then in medieval and Renaissance Europe (Clarke 1963). Ibn Sina (Avicenna) placed sensation, cognition, and movement in the brain, which he believed was controlled, in turn, by the heart (Gruner 1930). Basically, there are four kinds of intellect: (1) physical intelligence; (2) mental intelligence; (3) spiritual intelligence; and (4) emotional intelligence:

Kinds of Intellect

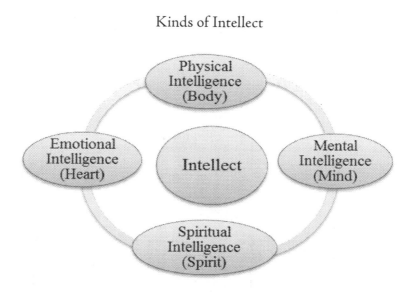

Physical intelligence is our ability to maintain and develop our physical fitness. It corresponds to *body*. Mental intelligence (or IQ) is our ability to analyze, reason, think abstractly, use language, visualize, and comprehend. It corresponds to *mind*. Spiritual intelligence is our drive for meaning and connection with the infinite. It corresponds to *spirit*. Emotional intelligence is our self-knowledge, self-awareness, social sensitivity, empathy, and ability to communicate successfully with others. It corresponds to *heart* (Covey 2006).

Covey illustrates how to develop a balanced life using these four intelligences:

+ Physical intelligence
  ○ wise nutrition
  ○ consistent balanced exercise
  ○ proper rest, relaxation, and stress management, and preventive thinking

+ Mental intelligence
  ○ continuous, systematic, disciplined study and education
  ○ cultivation of self-awareness (by making assumptions explicit)

- ○ learning by teaching and doing

- ✦ Spiritual intelligence
  - ○ making and keeping promises
  - ○ educating and obeying your conscience
  - ○ asking questions to yourself and living the answers

- ✦ Emotional intelligence
  - ○ being proactive
  - ○ beginning with the end in mind
  - ○ putting first things first
  - ○ thinking win/win
  - ○ seeking first to understand; then to be understood
  - ○ synergizing
  - ○ sharpening the saw

Whatever description of intelligence, the Qur'an lays great emphasis on the intellect:

> They will further say: "Had we but listened or used our intelligence, we should not (now) be among the companions of the Blazing Fire (Hell)!" (Qur'an 67:10)

This Qur'anic command ordering the use of the intellect is a fundamental religious obligation. The Qur'an admonishes the disbeliever who fails to reason and to mediate on the signs of God as unintelligent and irrational (Qur'an 38:29). As we are endowed with reason and accessibility to the reality of life, we should guard ourselves against the ego and immoral and flagrant desires by bringing into focus our emotional intelligence.

If our thoughts that affect our lives are hidden within the heart, then how can we come to know what we really think in our hearts? Is there a way that our unconscious thought reveals itself to us? The answer to this question lies in the emotional life. Our emotions are the direct way that we experience reality (Saucy 2013). Yet we do think, feel, and make choices from the heart. Research has shown that the heart can think.

Chapter 3

Heart Intelligence Testimonials

Undoubtedly the brain makes countless decisions and guides our behavior with astonishing speed and efficiency. However, the heart is also equipped to think and, at times, to give the brain orders instead of taking them. For example, when watching a horror movie, a person can observe the grotesque images on the screen more effectively as the heart contracts (pumping blood out to the body) than when observing them as the heart relaxes (taking blood in). Another example is when emotional feelings (heart) can delay the time it takes to make a decision, rather than making the decision solely based on logic (brain). Even when we shop for a new car based on having set criteria, such as pricing, specifications and options, we suddenly notice a blue convertible in the dealer's showroom that catches our interest. Against our better judgment, something emotionally deep inside of us—our hearts—says to buy it.

Emotions play a significant role in the way we buy and the way we convince ourselves to purchase something. Our brains tell us, *Why purchase another suit when there are already twenty suits hanging in my closet?* But the heart prevails, thinking how gorgeous this new outfit is and how it will add to our appearance. Our brains tell us not to believe everything we hear from politicians, but our hearts think otherwise as they are won over by passionate and heartfelt speeches.

In surveys of hundreds of US and Indian citizens conducted online via Amazon's Mechanical Turk website, the research team led by Adam Galinsky, at Columbia Business School, used a range of creative ways to establish whether someone is a heart person or a brain person. The participants in the surveys reflected more deeply than would a straightforward question and gave an indication of *how much* a person located his or her self in the heart versus the brain or other body part, rather than its being a simple either/or issue. For example, imagine you plan for various organs to be donated after you die so that your "self" lives on in these people. Imagine, too, that you had $100 million to bequeath to the different organ recipients—how would you distribute the money among them? The researchers found most people gave the lion's share of the money to the brain receiver and heart receiver, with only a small amount passed on to the receivers of the eyes, stomach, spine, and other parts. There was evidence that men are more often primarily brain-recipient than heart-recipient, whereas this bias was far weaker in women. The researchers also found that heart locators of either sex were more likely to endorse proposals for stricter abortion laws, based on the initial detection of a heartbeat in the fetus, and to endorse the idea that a person's death should be determined by when the heart stops beating rather than brain death. In a survey of college students, these same researchers further established that heart locators are more likely to support heart disease charities and that brain locators are biased toward brain-based charities; for example, an Alzheimer's disease charity.

In the same study, another finding was that those surveyed from India—a "collectivist culture"—were more likely to locate their selves in the heart. Moreover, the American students, prompted to reflect on their independence (by having them read a passage filled with pronouns like *me* and *I*), were more likely to locate their sense of self in the brain. Whereas when the researchers prompted students to think of their social interconnectedness with a passage filled with pronouns like *we* and *our*, the opposite was true. These participants were more likely to locate their sense of self in the heart (Jarrett 2015).

A heart donor was a three-year-old girl who drowned in the family pool. The recipient was a nine-year-old boy diagnosed with myocarditis and septal defect. The recipient's mother said:

> He [the recipient] doesn't know who his donor was or how she died. We do. She drowned at her mother's boyfriend's house. Her mother and her boyfriend left her with a teenage babysitter who was on the phone when it happened. I never met her father, but the mother said they had a very ugly divorce and that the father never saw his daughter. She said she worked a lot of hours and wished she had spent more time with her. I think she feels pretty guilty about it all ... you know, the both of them sort of not appreciating their daughter until it was too late.

The recipient, who claimed not to know who the donor was, reported:

> I talk to her sometimes. I can feel her in there. She seems very sad. She is very afraid. I tell her it's okay, but she is very afraid. She says she wishes that parents wouldn't throw away their children. I don't know why she would say that.

The recipient's mother said about the recipient:

> Well, the one thing I notice most is that Jimmy is now deathly afraid of the water. He loved it before. We live on a lake and he won't go out in the backyard. He keeps closing and locking the back door. He says he's afraid of the water and doesn't know why. He won't talk about it. (Brace 2006)

People make more moral decisions when they think their hearts are racing. A study of sixty-five students tested heart-monitoring equipment as they played a quick money-sharing game. They had to decide whether to instruct their partners, located in another room, to pick option A (which was more lucrative for the participant) or option B (more lucrative for the partner). Participants who heard their hearts beating fast were less likely to lie and tell their partners that they would be better off choosing option A (31 percent of them did so, compared with 58 percent of participants who heard their hearts beat at normal speed). This finding is consistent with Antonio Damasio's influential Somatic Marker hypothesis, which is based on the idea that bodily feedback guides our decisions, often at a nonconscious level. For example, people playing a card game sweat more when picking from the wrong, costly pile, even before they realize at a conscious level that it is the wrong choice. In addition, in another study, participants were less likely to volunteer their time after being given the chance to wash their hands, as if the process of physical cleansing left them feeling less need to compensate for past transgressions. What these studies revealed was that perceived physiological experiences play an important role in influencing moral behaviors; that is, listening to your heart may indeed shape ethical behaviors (Gu 2012).

In another study, research was done with the premise that the head is thought to be rational and cold, whereas the heart is thought to be emotional and warm:

> Eight studies of 725 participants pursued the idea that such body metaphors are widely consequential. Study 1 introduced a novel individual difference variable, one asking people to locate the self in the head or the heart. Irrespective of sex differences, head-locators characterized themselves as rational, logical, and interpersonally cold, whereas heart-locators characterized themselves as emotional, feminine, and interpersonally warm (Studies 1-3). Study 4 found that head-locators were more accurate in answering general knowledge questions and had higher GPAs and Study 5 found that heart-locators were more likely to favor emotional over rational considerations in moral decision-making. Study 6 linked

self-locations to reactivity phenomena in daily life – e.g., heart-locators experienced greater negative emotion on high stressor days. Study 7 manipulated attention to the head versus the heart and found that head-pointing facilitated intellectual performance, whereas heart-pointing led to emotional decision-making. Study 8 replicated Study 3's findings with a nearly yearlong delay between the self-location and outcome measures. The findings converge on the importance of head-heart metaphors for understanding individual differences in cognition, emotion, and performance. (Fetterman 2013)

Moreover, to substantiate these testimonials and endorsements of the heart's intelligence, I will explore the dynamics of the pure heart.

Chapter 4

Dynamics of the Pure Heart

How does the heart respond dynamically? The heart is alive and dynamic. Following is a comprehensive view of how thinking, feeling, and choosing are intricate dynamic heart responses.

Case Episode

A husband and wife have an argument over household expenses. The husband goes into a tirade, screaming and using foul language as he verbally insults his wife. She is speechless, almost in a state of shock, as she fears for her life. With anger and uncontrollable behavior, he continues to bombard her with expletives. These insults can only be described as wicked. In the heat of the argument, the husband starts to destroy the furniture by knocking down the television stand, upending the couch, and throwing chairs at his wife. Fortunately, they miss his wife but damage the wall. This outpouring of emotion lasts for over an hour and culminates with his kicking the front door, resulting in a huge dent. He leaves the house, but his wife is apprehensive, hysterical, and distressed.

Undoubtedly, this man's behavior is evil and sinful. Asking him to change is not wrong; helping him to understand those inner impulses as disturbing and frightening is not wrong either. The panacea for resolving this person's behavior is to explore the dynamics of the heart of which he may not be aware. Seeking the why rather than the what for his erratic outburst is a step in the right direction. Probing deep into the why of his anger can relate to his emotional view of life in general. For example, where does his anger lie within the husband-and-wife relationship? Why did he want to do harm? In the dynamics of his emotional instability we find a heart that believes, wants, and chooses something, and anger is a way of getting it. The husband needs to see what he needs—for example, self-awareness—in order to change. He needs to delve into the spiritual framework of the heart to understand how he experiences his family and the world in which he lives.

Thinking, feeling, and choosing are complex dynamic heart responses:

Dynamic Heart

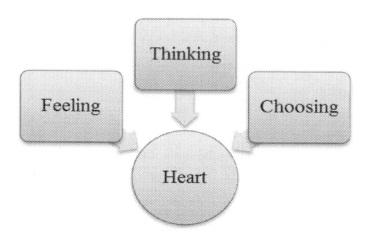

During the course of the day, we are confronted with numerous decisions to make. What we think, feel, or choose impacts these decisions, as each of these dynamics interact with each other. For example, the perceived value of our emotions is based on how we think, feel, or choose. We have feelings when we are sad or happy. Sadness or happiness is a feeling. Thinking determines what we can gain from that experience of being sad or happy. Choosing invokes us to make a decision as to how to overcome our sadness or extend our happiness.

The word *heart* is mentioned at least 130 times in the Qur'an. When mentioned, heart implies its thinking power. The heart and brain are dynamics, as each organ continuously influences the other's function. Our ability to hear and act on the information being sent from the heart can make the difference in whether we experience life as a series of stressful events or one that is rich in quality. The heart provides information that can help us eliminate the mental and emotional drain caused by confusion, stress, anxiety, and frustration:

> No kind of calamity can occur, except by the leave of God: and if any one believes in God, (God) guides his heart (aright): for God knows all things. (Qur'an 64:11)

Many benefits come from learning to utilize the heart's intelligence. They range from mental and emotional boosters, like more clarity, productivity, and creativity, to increased feelings of happiness (Friday sermon 2013).

Thinking from the heart is an experience we all need. Thinking from the heart will make us unite and embrace with emotion, without any illusions, doubts, analysis, ego, or judgment. It is higher than logic or reason and will enunciate the mind to transcend beyond its thought processes. If we separate the heart from the mind or allow one to rule, it is bound to oppose the other, leading to pain and conflict. The mind controls when we should be happy or sad. The mind even orders the heart how and when to express or suppress our emotions. Both cannot be left on their own. If the heart is on its own, it will only fantasize into emotions, hopes, and dreams. It is the union of both the heart and mind that leads us back to the oneness of ourselves (Kumar 2013). Therefore, we think with both our hearts and minds. However, unlike the mind, our hearts operate within their own orderly programming. It is the heart that drives our decisions, while the mind serves the heart in fulfillment of those decisions:

What! Have not they travelled in the earth that they should have hearts to understand them with, or ears to hear them with? For verily blind are not the eyes but blind are the hearts that are in their breasts. (Qur'an 22:46)

When we hear bad news, we might feel our hearts drop or have to deal with a heartache. While the heart is essential to our lives by supplying our body with blood, it is also the place where we experience many of our feelings.

The heart is recognized as the source of intelligence by Hebrew, Christian, Hindu, Chinese, and Islamic traditions. There is new scientific evidence that the heart organ is responsible for feelings and emotions. The heart uses neurological, biochemical, and biophysical ways to send emotional and intuitive signals to the brain. Scientists have discovered that the heart may be the actual intelligent force that is behind the intuitive thoughts, feelings, and emotions we experience. Emotions are connected with the rhythm of the heart. If we feel frustrated or nervous, we may notice that our heartbeats are irregular. If we took an electrocardiogram (EKG or ECG) test, it would show high irregular curves. In turn, if we feel loved or confident, the curves are more regular. This can help us to understand that the heart organ is responsible for feelings and emotions (Heart Doctor's World 2009).

According to a study, a link was found between the cycles of a beating heart and the likelihood of someone becoming frightened. Tests on healthy volunteers found that they were more likely to feel a sense of fear at the moment when their hearts contracted and pumped blood around their bodies, compared with the point when the heartbeat was relaxed. Scientists say the results suggest that the heart is able to influence how the brain responds to a fearful event, depending on its point in its regular cycle of contraction and relaxation. "Our results showed that if we see a fearful face during systole—when the heart is pumping—then we judge this fearful face as more intense than if we see the very same fearful face during diastole—when the heart is relaxed." The study was presented at the British Neuroscience Association Festival in London in 2013 (Connor 2013).

The brain is rational and usually makes a decision based on the facts presented. It plans and looks ahead, weighs up the pros and cons, and then follows the path that makes the most logical sense. Conversely, the heart is based on emotion in that we feel a choice or decision. Something inside of us is pulling in a direction, sometimes with no rhyme or reason. There usually is no logic, just our intuition telling us it is right. We are emotional beings. If we never allow ourselves to feel sad or angry, that energy stays in the body. It can build up and result in depression or general feelings of unhappiness (Bryce 2017).

The heart is where our intuition lies. It is the source that guides us. The heart is where our true self resides and knows what is best for us. In making a choice, our brains may tell us one thing while our hearts push us toward making a different choice. A study done by Dr. Jamin Halberstadt, Department of Psychology, University of Otago, New Zealand, revealed that impulsive decisions made with the heart have better results than those made with the head. The study claims that decisions based on gut instinct often lead to more accurate or higher-quality decisions than a careful, analytic approach. In this way, decision-making can be faster, simpler, and more accurate. Meanwhile, pondering at length and being more analytical can mask a natural and useful emotional reaction.

Dr. Halberstadt said, "There is evidence that judgments based on preference—choosing something you like—are better when made as a snap decision. When faced with choices, people make different decisions when they are asked to analyze and explain them to when they act impulsively. There is good evidence to suggest that preference judgments – choosing the things that you like – are better if you act on impulse. Research has shown that if you make a snap decision on choosing something, you are more likely to remain happy with it in the future than if you take an analytical approach." Some decisions are associated with emotions, and pondering for too long about these choices can lead to the wrong conclusions. He concludes that subjective decision-making is an enormously simplified and potentially superior tool, as compared with the more effortful analytic strategies (Daily Mail 2006).

Although the mind does have an impact on our major decisions, we have opted to consult our hearts in making these choices—for example, loving someone, career choice, where to live, vacationing, wedding, when to apologize, trusting someone, or getting a second opinion about our health. Undoubtedly, we can be burned or blessed when making a decision solely from the gut. Nevertheless, we do! This kind of heart-possessing intelligence is even confirmed, as illustrated in the next chapter, by the teachings of Islam.

Chapter 5

Case Examples of Emotional Intelligence

Undeniably, heart science has finally caught up with Islamic scripture. The teachings of Islam underscore the importance of emotions as fundamental elements of the human soul. As such, Islam emphasizes the importance of emotional intelligence in the Islamic code of conduct even more than it does hereditary intelligence (IQ). Following are four examples of emotional intelligence relative to leadership, conflict resolution, the Battle of Uhud, and the virtue of hope.

Leadership

Emotional intelligence has a strong impact on leadership. The core of high emotional intelligence is self-awareness. If you don't understand your own motivations and behaviors, it's nearly impossible to develop an understanding of others. While leadership is appropriate for those who manage companies or businesses, we, as Muslims, need to link ourselves to another kind of leadership: spiritual or Islamic leadership.

Here, leadership demands results and provides the courage to overcome ignorance, fear, and denial.

Leadership is about opening the heart. It comes from the heart and considers the heart of others. The style of leadership stimulates the intensity of motivation from within the heart. Nonetheless, during our lifetimes, our motivation is intensified by transformation of aspirations and a style of leadership that we develop. The aspect of empowerment augments these aspirations. As we strive for empowerment leadership, the leadership of domination and authority wears off. Empowerment is team motivated.

With empowerment, motivation is based on creativity. The qualities of this type of leader are of achievement and change. Conversely, domination and authority leadership is the principal style in our society because the majority of people resists and dislikes change. For example, the affairs of a mosque are run by tradition, and the members of the congregation prefer the status quo as opposed to change. This is a reason why many leaders from Islamic institutions find it difficult to cope with contemporary societies. True, many mosques are built with beautiful and remarkable architecture. However, it is neither the beauty nor the architecture of the mosque that brings out the good in Muslims; rather, it is the Muslims themselves. What is needed is a change in the minds and hearts of Muslims so as to become self-motivated and to take on Islamic responsibilities for the betterment of the individual, family, and community. Muslims are motivated by empowerment leadership, seeking out opportunities, challenges, and efficient and effective ways of building a more productive Islamic society.

The world is rapidly changing, due in large measure to the myriad advances in technology. Because of this, Muslims must be willing to learn and apply new skills, and they must work together to resolve problems. The self-actualized Muslim will adapt to this change within the context of Islamic ethics, morals, rules, and regulations. Muslims who want to advance the goals and objectives of a mosque are inspired in a team-motivated environment, whereby each person becomes a leader of his or her input.

Promoting leadership unity in a mosque is a challenge. Muslim goals should be proactive in the treatment of potential conflict, as well as understanding the inclinations of fellow Muslims. By working in faith groups at the mosque toward common principles, conflict becomes avoidable. Rather than being competitive, it is better to be complementary and cooperative with each other. This requires a commitment to develop more profound friendships and respect with other leaders in the mosque. Encouragement of a fellow leader can go a long way in building sound relationships.

Another issue is that family leadership is on a continual decline. Parents no longer enjoy the respect of their children that at one time was traditional and automatic, yet parents demand it. Respect can be achieved if it is a mutual respect between parents and children. Furthermore, parents must be pious, understanding, and righteous in order to set the example for their children. Oftentimes, parents demand respect, even though their own lifestyles are highly questionable. In Islam, cultural values must be in synchronization with religious values. The pure heart (*qalbun saleem*) embraces leadership that begins in the home, with parents acting as role models for their children. Proper planning between parents can help attain harmony and respect within the family.

If we look at the successes of healthy families, we find common characteristics. To begin with, rules are implemented, by which each family member must abide. There are no shortcuts, and mutual respect is the order of the day. High standards relative to attitude and behavior are established and implemented. When these standards are met, the children progressively instill powers of judgment and ethics. Rather than each family member taking on the authoritarian role of *me*, or the dictatorial role of *you*, it is more productive to function as *we*. This, in turn, reflects unity in the family. Moreover, the healthy family grows in character and faith as their pure hearts connect with each other.

Just as a business has a set of standards and rules, so must the family have a set of standards and rules. For example, a business operates within the framework of a mission statement, organizational structure, chain of command, budget requirements, and a set of performance objectives. Likewise, a family operates much the same way. If there is no chain of command in the family, then everyone is free to do as he or she wishes.

This presents a problem, as there is no accountability by anyone. The children, for example, could encounter serious problems in their lives. If there is no one to counsel or direct them, then the end result will be chaos.

Working together in the arena of *we* brings out a healthier framework and one that fosters structure within the family unit. Praying together as a family brings out the best in *we*, as God orders us to honor each other. In this way, leadership is built, nurtured, and promoted as each member of the family unit is reared in the direction of a vision, a purpose, and a design. Leadership in the family is one of shared views, priorities, communication, collaboration, and mutual respect. Creating an atmosphere of trust and truth are also vital to a family's healthy success. From another vantage point, leaders are like a rope—they can pull us up or drag us down. Prophet Mohammad and his progeny are like ropes that pull us up.

One cannot be an effective leader without genuine character. Prophet Mohammad and his progeny taught us about character, and the best of character is when we fully submit our will to the will of God and obey His commandments and the teachings of His messengers. We strive to become like the best of role models; that is, the Prophets and Infallible Imams. We try to imitate these role models and pattern our attitudes, behaviors, and lifestyles after them (Turfe 2004).

Conflict Resolution

Conflicts can be the result of political upheavals, social disputes, or cultural biases. We often lack the confidence or vision for what is appropriate to do. Many of us are under the assumption that conflict is something to be avoided. Many people view conflict as an experience of failure.

Over the centuries, attempts in trying to resolve the sectarian conflict between Sunnis and Shi'as only resulted in limited success because both sides did not have a genuine long-term solution. In effect, conflict resolution derived from the mind-set rather than from the emotional intelligence of the heart. Understanding similarities and differences, in an atmosphere free of bias that emanates from the pure heart, enables Muslim scholars and religious leaders to pursue in the direction of equality and justice. Attitudes and behaviors as well as environmental pressures can work toward a positive tolerance or a negative intolerance. It all depends on the mind-sets of these proponents, guided by the purity of heart and their willingness to work toward unity.

For conflict resolution to be effective, both sides of the conflict must be immersed within *qalbun saleem* (pure heart) by adhering to the following:

+ atmosphere of mutual respect and trust
+ reciprocal communication
+ promoting self-worth
+ free expression of ideas and thoughts
+ advancing scholarly questioning and methodical decision-making
+ promoting open-mindedness and regard for different points of view
+ deciding on an outcome after carefully considering alternatives
+ differentiating between rational behavior and emotional behavior

Conflicts are more than just a matter of ethics or morality. They have to do with myriad issues that are very complicated and difficult to resolve. However, at the center of many of these conflicts are the following:

+ preconception and narrow-mindedness
+ opposition and antagonism
+ absence of constructive criticism
+ disrespect for others

Preconceived notions result from ignorance and may be obstacles toward creating alternative solutions. Frequently, people do not get the chance to learn how to find alternative solutions or to develop constructive ways of resolving their conflicts. Learning to manage conflict without hostility can induce people toward sound communication. Conflict resolution rescues us from ignorance, and it is an important way to help people understand each other. Conflict resolution encourages people to be proactive and face conflict, not avoid it. The objective is to let the pure heart (*qalbun saleem*) reach a win/win situation with a remedy that is satisfactory to everyone involved.

Conflict resolution takes into account the feelings and emotional intelligence of all the people involved in a conflict. Conflict resolution is a solution toward generating empathy, reconciliation, candidness, and forgiveness. Reconciliation and conflict resolution initiatives require the identification of those Muslim leaders in the society who have the fortitude to seek social justice and peace. These Muslim leaders must move in the direction of unity, even if it means taking the ridicule visited upon them. Attitudes and behaviors of people are, in part, the reflection of their family values and states of mind. There needs to be a transformation of the inner heart in order to resolve deep-rooted conflicts.

Muslim brothers and sisters must build relationships by exercising empathy in their hearts in order to generate a common bond between the parties. For example, dialogue between devout Sunni and Shi'a Muslims could focus on the concept of empathy as a vehicle for understanding the needs and concerns of each other. Walking in their shoes and seeing the perspective from their vantage point can help to understand the feelings of the other party.

Battle of Uhud

Prophet Muhammad knew the importance of recognizing the emotions of his followers in order to keep them in balance and united.

> Thus, it is a mercy of God that thou are lenient unto them: had thou been severe and hard-hearted, they would surely have dispersed away from around thee; therefore, forgive them and seek pardon for them; and take their counsel in the affair; but when thou are resolved, then

put thou thy trust in God; for God loves those who trust (in Him). (Qur'an 3:159)

The meaning of this verse can be illustrated by the Battle of Uhud—some of the Muslims broke their promise to Prophet Muhammad by escaping to take shelter on the mountain, and others actually deserted from the battle scene. Prophet Muhammad's army consisted of one thousand men versus three thousand men for the enemy. However, one-third of the Prophet's army returned back to Medina at the behest of Abdullah bin Ubay, who was a staunch critic of the Prophet in Medina. Hence, the Muslims suffered a setback at the Battle of Uhud because of their lack of patience.

During the battle, Prophet Muhammad's soldiers suffered a great loss because the archers disobeyed his orders; they moved too soon from their strategic post on a hilltop in order to hurriedly collect the spoils of war that lay on the plains below. As a result, the Prophet's position was defenseless, and so the enemy attacked from the rear, eventually causing the Muslims to withdraw. The Muslims forgot that their goal was to defeat the aggressors and establish the truth. They learned a valuable lesson on the importance of obeying the Prophet at all times, including when their desires for booty, wealth, power, or other material gain in this world attempted to thrust them to do otherwise. The Prophet had instructed his archers to remain in their post no matter what happened. They left their post, however, thinking that the enemy had turned away from the battlefield. Even when their commander reminded them of the Prophet's order not to leave their post, they did not listen. As a result, the Prophet was severely wounded, and many of his companions were martyred (Turfe 2016).

The deserters actually deserved to be punished. Even though they were granted a pardon, there is no room for them to say they deserved it or that they were honorably acquitted of the charges against them. The blot of conviction remains there.

The reason the pardon was given is in the above verse: "had thou been severe and hard-hearted, they would surely have dispersed away from around thee." Therefore, the Prophet was made lean-hearted toward them; otherwise, the people would not have cared to stay around him, and the whole scheme of guidance and salvation of humankind would have come to an end (S. V. Mir Ahmed Ali 1995). In addition, Islam at that time was still new to the people and not firmly solidified in their minds as to what was expected of them, relative to the code of conduct; therefore, the reason for the pardon. Furthermore, the concept of *qalbun saleem* (pure heart) had not been firmly established yet in the hearts of those who deserted. As the Prophet knew the emotional state of these deserters, he was the ideal example of emotional expression—when and how to express emotions—with the ultimate objective of developing their emotional intelligence.

What we learn from the experience at the Battle of Uhud is that Islam provides a framework whereby a whole range of human emotions are recognized and respected. We have our weak moments and exhibit such emotions as desertion, anger, jealousy, intolerance, and fragmentation. As we experience bad emotions, we still make a serious effort to regain our balance and composure in order to be in compliance with the Islamic personality. It is the pure heart (*qalbun saleem*) that brings us into balance with the Islamic personality. Our Infallible Imams give us the reasons.

Imam Ja'far as-Sadiq said,

> The heart possesses two ears; the spirit of belief slowly invites him towards righteous deeds, while the Satan slowly invites him towards evil deeds. Therefore, whoever becomes victorious in this struggle takes over heart's control. (Bihar al-Anwar, vol. 70, p. 53)

> The darkness of the heart is the worst kind of darkness. (*Bihar al-Anwar*, vol. 70, p. 51)

Imam Mohammad al-Baqir said,

> There is nothing worse than sinning for the heart. When the heart is encountered with sin, it struggles against the

sin until sin becomes victorious thus making the heart as a reversed heart. (*Bihar al-Anwar*, vol. 70, p. 54)

There are three kinds of hearts: First Type: Reversed heart that lacks feelings for any sort of righteous deeds. Such heart is the heart of an unbeliever. Second Type: The heart that contains a black spot in which a war is being waged between the truth and falsehood and whichever becomes victorious will take over the heart's control. Third Type: The conquered heart in which there is a lighted lamp that is never going to be turned off. Such a heart is the heart of a believer. (*Bihar al-Anwar*, vol. 70, p. 51)

Initially there is a white spot and light within the heart of a human being and as a result of his committing sin, a black spot appears. If the person repents, the black spot gets wiped out, but if he persisted in sinning, the blackness gradually increases ultimately covering the entire white spot; when this happens, the owner of such a heart will never return towards goodness and become manifestation of the verse of the Holy Qur'an: "Nay, but that which they have earned is rust upon their hearts." (*Al-Kafi*, vol. 2, p. 273)

Abu Hudhaifah, in *Sahih Muslim*, said,

"I heard the Messenger of God say: 'Tribulations will stick to people's hearts like the fibers of a reed mat, one by one. Any heart that imbibes them will get a black spot, and any heart that rejects them will get a white spot, until there will be two types of hearts. One will be white like a smooth stone, which will not be harmed by any tribulation so long as heaven and earth endure. And the other will be black and gloomy, like an overturned vessel, not acknowledging any goodness nor rejecting any evil, except what suits its own whims and desires.'" (*Sahih Muslim*, vol. 1, book 1, chapter 64, Hadith 369)

Imam Ali Zein al Abideen (Imam al-Sajjad) said,

> A man possesses four eyes, with two apparent eyes he sees the affairs relevant to his world, and with two esoteric eyes sees the affairs related to the next world. Therefore, whenever God desired the good for a believer, He opens his heart's eyes to enable him to witness the hidden world and its mysteries. But when He doesn't desire his welfare, leaves the heart with his esoteric eyes closed. (*Bihar al-Anwar*, vol. 70, p. 53)

Imam Ali ibn Abi Talib said,

> Everyone who lacks self-restraint and piety will have a dead heart; whoever has a dead heart will enter inside the Hell. (*Nahjul Balagha*, Saying #324)

> O my son! The poverty is one of the most horrible calamities. But still severe than poverty is the bodily sickness; and the sickness of soul is harsher than the bodily sickness. Plenty of wealth is one of God's blessings, but sound health is better than that, and the piety of heart is even superior to sound health. (*Bihar al-Anwar*, vol. 70, p. 51)

Virtue of Hope

Positive emotions such as hope and love are strongly encouraged in the Qur'an and the teachings of Prophet Muhammad, as they result in a positive attitude for Muslims. Islam regulates emotional balance as it encourages us to take hold of our emotional experiences, no matter how difficult they may be. For example, patients afflicted with life-threatening diseases seek cures for their ailments. At times, these patients are sapped of energy and become very tired. They become highly distressed and outright scared to death. For a long period of time, even years, they have taken the necessary medical treatments and medicines but to no avail. They turn to hope in their dire state of hopelessness. A study investigated the role of emotional intelligence in predicting a sense of humor and hope among adults (Batool 2014).

Research indicates that emotional intelligence has an association with hope, which helps to have an optimistic outlook on the future. Hope is a mind-set that is based on a reciprocally resulting sense of positive thinking. Hope is closely linked with emotional intelligence because people who have a low level of hope are unable to adjust mentally; thus, emotionally they have no ability to learn from their illness and cannot make the future better. Researchers also proved that people with a high level of hope show emotional passion, while those with a lower level of hope show emotional tiredness (Snyder 2002).

Hope is sought through spiritual prayer and meditation. Spirituality is experienced and guided by cultural traditions and religious doctrine (DuBray 2001). Living a spiritual life and/or having a strong faith can positively impact not only the course of a chronic disease or terminal illness but also how that disease or illness is perceived (Sorajjakool and Lamberton 2004). All hope is not lost. For example, research demonstrates that religious practices such as worship attendance and prayer may contribute to physical and emotional health. Although the studies have not demonstrated a cause-and-effect relationship, there is strong evidence of an important connection between religious practice and good health (Fontaine 2000). In addition to turning to medical care for healing, people also turn to prayer. Even when physical healing does not occur, some degree of improvement almost always takes place, most often a sense of peace in facing a serious illness or disability (Matthews and Clark 1998).

Hope and emotional intelligence are valuable traits for leading a practical and professional life. While emotional intelligence helps to maintain positive mood, it also has been found to be associated with sense of humor, which assists in coping with stress and emotional expression. A positive humor style is related to a high level of emotional intelligence, if only individuals desire to understand their emotions and emotions of others. On the other hand, people who use negative styles of humor also may have a lower level of emotional intelligence, but they don't have awareness and understanding of emotions (Vernon 2008).

There is always hope, if we put our trust in God.

> Whosoever fears (*the wrath of*) God, He will make for him a way (*out of the troubles*), and provide him with sustenance from whence he reckoned not; and whosoever relies on God, then sufficient is He for him. (Qur'an 65:2–3)

> God will soon bring about ease after difficulty. (Qur'an 65:7)

> Verily, with (*every*) difficulty (*there*) is ease. Verily, with (*every*) difficulty (*there*) is ease. (Qur'an 94:5–6)

> And lose you not heart and grieve you not, for you shall gain the upper hand, if you (*only*) be (*true*) believers. (Qur'an 3:139)

While much of hope lives in the mind, faith is steeped in the heart and soul. The hearts of true believers, like my sister Hajjah Wanda Fayz, is immersed in the constant hope of God's kindness, generosity, and favors. True believers are optimistic, never losing hope in the bounty of God that He bestows on whom He wills. Constantly performing good deeds and remembering God ensures that our hope will be answered. Trust (*tawakkul*) in God, and never lose hope. With a contented heart, believers will always remain hopeful, as faith and hope are interrelated.

Chapter 6

The Contented Heart

While God provides us with His mercy and kindness, some people fail to see the purpose of God and doubt He will provide for the future. They doubt the love and goodness of God. They are discontented with God and lose perspective of the eternal. These are signs of the discontented heart.

We live in a world that breeds discontent. We are overwhelmed with messages that to be happy we need to look younger, feel energetic, purchase more goods, and have more vacations and fewer problems. In today's society, people are constantly trying to slip into imaginary worlds, to forget about life and its problems. Life is so pressurized, to the point that people literally look for some form of escape. There is disconnect in society in that people are disengaged at work, at home, at mosques, in their marriages, with their children, and with life itself. People also become bored of their pastimes and constantly search for new ones.

How different are the ways of the Qur'an from the trends of modern society. The Qur'an does not hide itself from reality but faces it directly. The Qur'an puts meaning into life and gives us a sense of accomplishment and satisfaction. Ultimately, however, the problem is the sinful heart.

The Qur'an teaches us that we need to implant contentment within our hearts to overcome transgressions.

Qalbun saleem (pure heart) is also known as the contented heart. Contentment (*qana'a*) is the awareness of sufficiency, a sense that we have enough, and we are enough, and we appreciate the simple gifts of life. Those who find contentment always are satisfied. Contentment offers happiness regardless of our adversity, hardship, or even financial problems. While the pursuit of wealth is good, it should not control us.

People seem to think that the pursuit of wealth and material things improves their enjoyment in life. If this is their rationale, then it is flawed. However, if they feel that enhancing their financial status can be used for charitable purposes, such as feeding the poor and tending to the needs of the orphans, then that premise is not flawed but encouraged. The truth is that once their basic needs are met, then the pursuit of more money contributes little to their overall happiness and well-being. Therefore, the virtue of contentment itself is one of great wealth.

People have a tendency to be overly impatient, as they want more money, goods, and answers to their problems right this instant! Sometimes, knowing everything immediately can be uncontrollable and can impact us adversely. Our tendency is that while we want change in our lives, for example, to enhance our financial status, we don't want to wait for it. However, God has offered us the great gift of patience (*sabr*) to strengthen and protect our contentment during the waiting process. With *sabr*, we feel completely satisfied, lacking nothing.

Prophet Joseph waited a very long time to fulfill his dream that God had given him. During that time, Prophet Joseph had the patience to wait and the contentment to be happy, knowing God would respond. The lesson learned here is that those who are in constant pursuit of worldly pleasures and materialism eventually will collapse because they do not possess the faith that enables them to persevere during tough times.

Those who have strong faith during tough times—such as the loss of a loved one, an unfortunate accident, or being afflicted with an incurable illness—will remain patient and steadfast in coping with these adversities. They have conditioned themselves via the contented heart (*qalbun saleem*) to face these afflictions with a tranquil disposition. Man is a maximizing being, in that he will always prefer more of something than less of it. Not being fully satisfied, he thinks about losing that which he desires or the greed for more wealth. Such a person transgresses, becomes arrogant, and never has peace of mind. He is constantly restless, disturbed, and discontented. Contentment, however, is a blessing from God that strengthens our faith and brings about peace and joy to those who have it,

> It is He Who sent down tranquility (contentment) into the hearts of the believers, that they might add faith to their faith. (Qur'an 48:4)

We experience the contented heart (*qalbun saleem*) in good times as well as in bad times.

Contented Heart

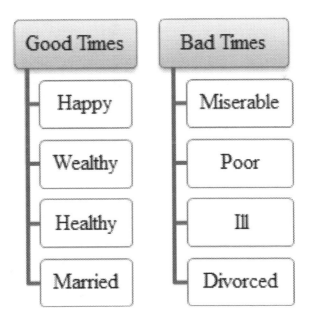

Being content doesn't mean that we are always happy, wealthy, healthy, or married. We also are content when we are miserable, poor, ill, or divorced. Contentment is about being happy with who we are. For example, the secret of happiness is manifested in righteousness. To be righteous we must develop a sense of optimism and trust, as well as a positive outlook on creation. To be righteous is to be content, and to be content is to be happy.

Contentment also derives from empathy, as we feel for the poor and reflect on their needs. We can develop contentment by being grateful for what we have because others may have less. American statesman Benjamin Franklin said, "Content makes poor men rich; discontent makes rich men poor" (Franklin 2010). True contentment isn't something that we find in circumstances; rather, it is only found in our convictions. Our trust in God's mercy and beneficence is sufficient for us in all circumstances, both good and bad. Contentment leads to being grateful (*shukr*) to God. Contentment and those who blindly follow their own desires cannot coexist in the same heart.

Unfortunately, many people lack contentment. Those who achieve success may not find contentment. They are driven to want more and are unhappy with themselves. They have goods that meet their needs, but they always want an upgrade to a nicer, more expensive version of a house, car, jewelry, or clothes. Driving a Chevrolet meets their need for transportation, but driving a Cadillac would enhance their social status. Likewise, moving to a bigger, more luxurious house uplifts their status as well. The desire to be wealthy, famous, and powerful also leads to discontentment. The end result is a bitter life of rivalry, greed, and jealousy.

Rather than thanking God for what they already have, they think more about material and worldly status. Imam Ja'far as-Sadiq said, "If a son of Adam possessed two vast valleys wherein gold and silver flowed, he would still wish to search for a third one" (*Man La Yahduruhul Faqih*, vol. 4, p. 418). Advertising and promotional schemes play a big role in luring them into wanting more and more, rather than just being content with what they already have. In effect, they are overly ambitious, miserable, and unhappy because they always want more. On the other hand, many people who are poor or don't have a successful career have found contentment. Hence, those who are content are very wealthy because they don't feel they need anything more.

Contentment is a journey of the heart at peace. Trusting ourselves is the key because without trust, it's difficult to be content. At times, we have low self-worth in that we judge ourselves badly. In addition, we compare ourselves to something that may be unrealistic. For example, while we want to look physically attractive, drive luxurious cars, be the captain of a high school sports team, become multilingual, have the perfect spouse and children, and lead an astonishing social life, these things may not be attainable, even though they are realistic goals. As a result, we become discontented because we don't measure up to these ideals.

To find contentment is to stop comparing and judging ourselves by these ideals or to other people. Jealousy and comparison are major factors of discontentment. Stop comparing yourself to delusions of grandeur, magnificence, and glory. Don't be self-judgmental, surrounded with false impressions and negative beliefs that may leave irreparably deep scars. Learn to trust your heart and be contented with who you really are. The contented heart brings about happiness as we find internal and external peace, free of confusion, turmoil, and unrest. The contented heart is an investment that gives us peace, harmony, and connectivity to God.

Prophet Muhammad said, "Look for your heart in three places: when listening to the Qur'an, when seeking knowledge (of God), and when in privacy. If you cannot find it in these places, then ask God to bless you with a heart, for indeed you have no heart" (Al-Jawziyyah 2017).

> Verily, believers are only those who when God is mentioned their hearts get   thrilled, and when unto them are recited His signs they increase them in faith, and on God (*alone*) do they rely, those who establish prayer and of what God has provided them with, they spend (*benevolently in the way of their Lord*). (Qur'an 8:2)

> Read thou! (*O' Our Apostle Muhammad!*) In the name of thy Lord Who created (*everything in the Universe*). (Qur'an 96:1)

Prophet Muhammad said, "One hour of your contemplation is better than seventy years of worship." (*Dastan-ha Wa Pand-ha*, vol. 5, p. 87; *Tafsir Ruhul Bayan*, vol. 8, p. 440)

These three places of the contented heart or pure heart are intensified as we examine and discuss its virtues.

Chapter 7

Virtues of the Pure Heart

Qalbun saleem is Arabic for pure heart. *Qalbun* means heart or mind, while *saleem* denotes pure, healthy, sound, safe, submissive, or good. Literally, *qalbun saleem* means healthy heart, submissive heart, or sound mind. *Qalbun saleem* derives from the following verses in the Qur'an:

> The Day when will avail not wealth or sons, save him who comes unto God with a heart submissive. (Qur'an 26:88–89)

> When came he unto his Lord with a submissive heart. (Qur'an 37:84)

In the first verse, God informs us that neither our wealth nor our sons are going to be of any benefit to us on the Day of Judgment, except that we bring to God a pure heart. God does not look at our outer beauty and adornments; rather, He looks at our actions, righteous deeds, and purity of our hearts. In the second verse, God describes Prophet Abraham as one who came to his Lord with a pure heart. In destroying the imagery of false idols, Prophet Abraham was the compass that guided his people to the straight path in worshipping only God.

Qalbun saleem is a heart that is pure and unaffected by the moral ills that afflict others. It is a personal condition that is free from bad characteristics that are both personally and socially dangerous. Being pure, *qalbun saleem* is full of good characteristics and motivation. We free our minds from any bad thoughts and characteristics in order to adopt a high degree of good character. We free ourselves from bad characteristics such as arrogance, inferiority, prejudice, or envy, as well as other immoral and depraved traits. Being free from such bad character traits, we make every attempt to adopt high standards of personal qualities that are necessary to achieve a pure heart, *qalbun saleem*. The very basis for *qalbun saleem* is a strong grasp of *tawhid* (oneness of God). As there is only one God in which to believe, we totally rely on Him. Based on this total conviction of the oneness of God, we attribute all our good traits to the inspiration of Islam (Solahudin 2008).

While *qalbun saleem* (pure heart) consists of many virtues and criteria, its essence is the belief in God. While people who disbelieve in God may have a sincere heart, perform good deeds, and have compassion for humankind, which are also requisites for a pure heart, these people do not fall within the criteria of what constitutes *qalbun saleem*. In the pure heart, there is no substitute for the belief in God. According to a survey conducted by the Pew Research Center in 2014, the majority of Americans still believe in God. However, the trend is pointing toward a decline in that belief and an upward swing by those who do not believe in God.

Declining Share of Belief in God by Americans

Belief in God	2007	2014	% Point Change
Certainty of Belief in God	92%	89%	-3
Absolute Certainty of Belief in God	71%	63%	-8

Don't Believe in God	5%	9%	+4

Source: 2014 Religious Landscape Study, conducted June 4— September 30, 2014 (Pew Research Center).

Americans who are certain of their belief in God declined from 92 percent in 2007 to 89 percent in 2014, a drop of three percentage points. Those who are absolutely certain of their belief in God also declined from 71 percent in 2007 to 63 percent in 2014, a drop of eight percentage points. Americans who don't believe in God increased by four percentage points, from 5 percent in 2007 to 9 percent in 2014.

The Pew study also disclosed that 84 percent of Muslim Americans are absolutely certain of their belief in God, 12 percent are fairly certain, and 3 percent are not too certain. Interestingly, the absolute certainty of belief in God by Muslim Americans rose two percentage points from the 82 percent level in 2007.

By comparison, 76 percent of Christian Americans are absolutely certain of their belief in God, 18 percent fairly certain, and 4 percent are not too certain. In contrast, 37 percent of Jewish Americans are absolutely certain, 27 percent are fairly certain, 15 percent are not too certain, and 17 percent do not believe in God.

The most alarming finding in the Pew study was that while 70 percent of Americans aged sixty-five or older expressed an absolute certainty of God's existence, only half of adults under the age of thirty felt the same way (51 percent) (Michael Lipka, "Americans' Faith in God May Be Eroding," Senior Editor, Pew Research Center, November 4, 2015).

In another study conducted by the Gallup Poll in May 2017, 87 percent of Americans believe in God, while 12 percent don't believe in God. However, for the May 2014 period (same time frame as the Pew study), the Gallup Poll numbers were 86 percent who believe in God and 11 percent who don't believe in God, but for the May 2011 period, the numbers were 92 percent and 7 percent, respectively (Gallup Poll Social Series, http://www.gallup.com/poll/1690/religion.aspx). This upward trend points to a steady surge in the disbelief of God by Americans.

In order to self-actualize in *qalbun saleem*, we must embrace and be totally absorbed in the virtues of remembrance (*dhikr*), patience (*sabr*), devotion (*ikhlas*), humility (*tawadhu'*), and honesty (*saraha*).

Virtues of Qalbun Saleem

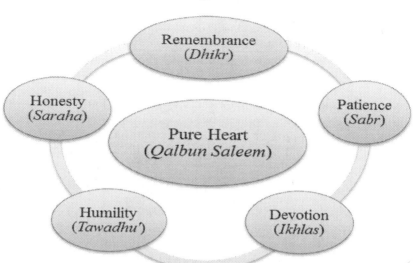

The Qur'an has mentioned the importance of the heart relative to the *dhikr* (remembrance) of God. Illnesses of the heart result from desires and doubts, and the Qur'an is a cure for both. The heart cures the diseases of desires that distort knowledge, understanding, and perception by enabling us to see things as they really are.

> And those who believe and their hearts are set at rest by God's remembrance. Certainly! By God's remembrance (*only*) are the hearts set at rest. (Qur'an 13:28)

> What! Is he whose breast (*heart*) God has opened for Islam then he follows the Light from God (like unto the hardhearted one)? Nay! Woe unto those whose hearts are hard against the remembrance of God (*dhikr*); those are in a clear error. (Qur'an 39:22)

There is a linkage between *dhikr* and Islam. When there is *dhikr* of

God, there is Islam, and where there is absence of *dhikr*, there is absence of Islam. When there is hardness in the heart, it can only be softened by *dhikr*. *Dhikr* is the remedy of the ills of the heart, thereby leading it to contentment. Praising God by words from the tongue is insufficient, as it must also be done in connection with remembrance (*dhikr*) of God in the heart.

> Imam Ali said, "Certainly, fear of God is the medicine for your hearts, sight for the blindness of your spirits, the cure for the ailments of your bodies, the rectifier of the evils of your breasts, the purifier of the pollution of your minds, the light of the darkness of your eyes, the consolation for the fear of your hearts, and the brightness for the gloom of your ignorance." (*Nahjul Balagha*, Sermon 197)

Having "fear of God" means protecting yourself from God's punishment by carrying out what God has commanded and abstaining from what God has prohibited. Just as it is expected that the tongue and heart will remain in a state of perpetual *dhikr*, so it is also imperative for the body as a whole to be engaged in *dhikr*.

Inner performance of *dhikr* depends on the condition of the heart. What is important in *dhikr* is not just the action of the tongue but that of the heart as well. By just reciting God's name, the tongue helps *dhikr* settle deep in the heart, whereupon the heart participates in the *dhikr*. When *dhikr* takes the heart under its control, it enlightens all feelings of one with heavenly light. When the heart is deprived of *dhikr*, the soul is devoid of love. When the heart is rusted for not remembering God and goes astray from the divine path, its only cure is *dhikr*. *Dhikr* polishes the heart and surrounds the heart, shining with God's light. The most important outcome of *dhikr* is the purification of the heart (Tenik 2008).

While *dhikr* is the key to success (*miftah al-falah*), *sabr* (patience) is the key of relief (*miftah al-faraj*). *Sabr* transcends into what we call *taqwah* (consciousness of God). Thereafter, everything we do is *kurbatan illallah* (to become nearer to God). Without *sabr*, we are like ships lost at sea, never knowing which direction to turn. *Sabr* is the compass that directs and guides us to the *dhikr* of God in order to reach the *sirat-al-mustaqim* (straight path). God is near those who have *dhikr* and *sabr*.

> Then you remember Me, I will remember you. Be grateful to Me, and do not reject faith. O you who believe? Seek help with patient perseverance and prayer: for God is with those who patiently persevere. (Qur'an 2:152–153)

The essential elements that bring about the tranquil and calm heart are *dhikr* (remembrance), *shukr* (gratitude), and *sabr* (patience). A heart that remains grateful (*shukr*) and patient (*sabr*) while in the remembrance (*dhikr*) of God will always be at peace. *Sabr* is mentioned before prayer because prayer cannot be firmly established without sabr. Our prayers also fill our hearts with the *dhikr* of God. After *dhikr* of God, *shukr* and *sabr*, the Qur'an places love of God as an important resource, for only such love makes faith (*iman*) real and meaningful.

With devotion through individual self-refinement (*tazkiya*) of our souls, we secure our faith through devotion (*ikhlas*) to God (i.e., absolute reliance on and acting only for the sake of God).

> Say: "Verily my prayer and my sacrifice, my life and my death (*are all, only devoted*) for God, the Lord of the worlds." (Qur'an 6:162)

Our reliance (*tawakkul*) on God guides us to the straight path and manifests itself in seeking God's contentment (*qana'a*), gratitude (*shukr*), generosity (*infaq*), and patience (*sabr*). We seek *tawakkul* by complete obedience and devotion to God. This devotion takes the shape of piety (*taqwah*), love, and loyalty to God. Devotion to God is worship and belief. Devotion is sincerity, and to be sincere we need to come to the defense of the Qur'an against those who would aspire to corrupt, abuse, and misinterpret it. We must be devoted to God and Prophet Muhammad and obey all of their commands and prohibitions. Whatever comes our way by Prophet Muhammad comes from God. *Ikhlas* is when our intention is to be devoted to God and obedient to God. The essence of *ikhlas* is when the heart is free of everything except God.

> Yet was not enjoined on them but that they should worship God (*alone*) in perfect sincerity (*devotion*), in religion (*only*) unto Him, and that they give away the poor-rate, and that is the religion (*correct and*) strong. (Qur'an 98:5)

Whatever we do, whatever task we undertake or relationship we make, our devotion is to always seek God. We must rid our hearts of false pretenses that are an impediment to the straight path that connects with God. In order to accomplish this act of devotion, we seek God first and thereafter everything else that is pure. It is devotion (*ikhlas*) to God that Satan cannot deceive.

> He (*Satan*) said: "My Lord! Because Thou has left me to stray, certainly will I adorn unto them the path of error, and certainly will I cause them all to go astray, save Thy (*devoted*) servants, of them the freed ones." (Qur'an 15:39–40)

Cognition (*ma'rifah*) emanates from both the mind recognizing faith in God and the heart's devotion in remembrance (*dhikr*) of God. As faith and devotion increase, so does cognition (*ma'rifah*). The devotion of the heart, which includes all the feelings and intentions of the mind, is indeed absolutely necessary at all times and under all external experiences. The numerous praises of God pronounced by the tongue would be but empty sounds without the devotional feelings of the heart. Furthermore, we must guard our tongues from uttering foul and disdainful words.

> The Messenger of God said: "Have you not heard? God does not punish for the tears of the eye or the grief of the heart, rather He punishes for this" – and he pointed

to his tongue – "or shows mercy (because of it)." (*Sahih Muslim*, vol. 2, book 11, chapter 6, Hadith 2137)

Another component of *qalbun saleem* is humility (*tawadhu'*). Humility is to be humble and aware of our nothingness before God. A person may have been given knowledge, position, and property. However, as a result, he must not oppress others, either physically or spiritually, who have been deprived of such things and claim to be superior to them.

"And be kind unto him who follows thee, of the believers" (Qur'an 26:215).

The humble person is generous. The generous person is compassionate. The compassionate person is full of joy and enthusiasm in serving others in order to attain the Lord's pleasure. A person who is distant from humility is deprived of all of these beautiful traits. Because discernment and insight develop in the humble person, he or she can then distinguish between friend and foe. Humility is a very important trait as it beautifies a person, matures him or her in serving God, and brings form to the person's character (Topbas 2009). *Tawadhu'* is calm and simple and a part of the noble character. Do not transgress, and be humble to your parents.

> And the servants of the Beneficent (*God*) are they who walk on the earth humbly; and when address them the ignorant, say they: salaam (*peace*). (Qur'an 25:63)

> Call you on your Lord, humbly and secretly; verily God does not love the transgressors. (Qur'an 7:55)

> And lower unto them the wing of humility out of compassion, and say thou: "O' My Lord! Have mercy on them as they cherished me when I was little." (Qur'an 17:24)

Tawadhu' is the quality or state of being humble and constant in humility. It is the opposite of arrogance, pride, and haughtiness. It means being not assuming, not pretentious, insignificant, and lowly. One should try to be humble and never act too proud. Humility is the portal to good conduct or being characterized with the qualities of God (such as generosity, merciful, helpful, and forgiving). It is first and foremost being near to Creator, and that nearness is manifested in prostrating before God in prayer. For example, Imam Ali ibn Abi Talib was humble and detested showiness (pretension) and conceit (haughtiness, pride, superiority, vanity, and self-importance). Even as caliph, he would sweep the floor of his own house, chop wood for fuel, carry water on his shoulders, mend his own shoes, wash his own clothes, and milk his goat. Imam Ali's wife, Fatima, did similar domestic jobs with her own hands, grinding wheat in the hand mill, baking bread, lighting the oven, washing the dishes, and tending to her children (Syed).

To be humble in the heart is to be submissive to the essence of *qalbun saleem*. It involves being more interested in serving the needs of others than in having our own needs met. The humble heart is cognizant of the needs of others and is willing to sacrifice so that others can benefit. The best way to achieve humbleness in the heart is to follow the example of Prophet Muhammad, who prescribed many methods to teach his companions how to be humble, such as to feed the poor and to extend peaceful greetings (*salaam*) to those we know, as well as to those we do not know. The essence of humility is helping those in need, like the poor, the orphans, and the indigent, in order to transform and soften the heart. Cultivating the humility in our hearts is to cleanse the heart from enmity and arrogance and from looking down upon others.

> The Prophet used to say ... O God! Cleanse my heart with the water of snow and hail, and cleanse my heart from all sins as a white garment is cleansed from filth, and let there be a far away distance between me and my sins as You made the east and west far away from each other. (*Sahih Bukhari*, vol. 8, book 80, chapter 46, Hadith 6377)

> The Prophet would supplicate: O Lord! Accept my repentance, and cleanse my sins, and respond to my supplication, and make firm my evidence, and guide my heart, and correct my tongue, and remove the evils (hatred and anger) of my heart. (*Sunan Abu Dawood*, vol. 2, book 8, chapter 25, Hadith 1510)

With humility and self-sacrifice, we can recover our sense of worth and regain spirituality, free of pride and complacency. Pray with humility both in the mental state and physical manner. Pray with hope and reverence, asking God for His mercy and forgiveness. Muslims from all over the world gather together in unity and humility to purify their faith through prayer. They seek to cleanse themselves of their worldly weaknesses that inhibit their steadfastness and self-sacrifice to God.

Another quality of *qalbun saleem* is honesty (*saraha*). *Qalbun saleem* is a pure heart that is free from lies and deception. The core of honesty is when we are truthful under all circumstances, fulfill our promise, and give sound, untainted advice to those who ask for it.

Honesty incorporates the concepts of truthfulness and reliability, and it resides in all human thoughts, words, actions, and relationships. It is more than just accuracy; it is more than just truthfulness; it denotes integrity or moral soundness.

> O' you who believe! Fear you God and be you (*always*) with the truthful ones. (Qur'an 9:119)

Honesty is an essential ingredient of the Muslim character, including being truthful toward God by worshipping Him sincerely; being truthful to ourselves by adhering to God's laws; and being truthful with others by speaking the truth and being honest in all dealings. A true Islamic society is based upon honesty and justice and is intolerant of dishonesty in all of its manifestations (Stacey 2008). Telling the truth is a key for all doors of goodness that may lead to paradise.

Verily forge the lie only they who believe not in the signs of God, and these, they are the liars. (Qur'an 16:105)

God will say: "This is the day when shall benefit the truthful ones; their truth for them shall be gardens beneath which rivers flow to abide therein forever; God is well pleased with them and they are well pleased with God; this is the great achievement." (Qur'an 5:119)

Honesty attracts honesty. Those who are trustworthy and honest attract others who are trustworthy and honest. Healthy societies are marked by people who are honest, sincere, and dependable and whose deeds match their words. As honesty is a virtue, if all people in a society became honest, then the society will be an ideal society. Although a utopian type of an ideal society may not be attainable, we still make every effort to try to reach it. Toward this end, remaining honest becomes our goodwill in life. Honesty is at the very heart of spirituality. Honesty in the heart speaks to behavior and character in order to avoid deceiving and lying to others as well as to ourselves. An honest heart is interested in the truth and will examine oneself upon hearing the truth to ensure proper ethics and moral compliance. The honest heart holds fast to the *Rope of God* and is not divided. Holding fast transforms into uniting our hearts in friendship and love, so by God's favor we become brethren.

The question arises: what is the state of our hearts relative to these virtues of remembrance, patience, devotion, humility, and honesty? How do we benefit from these virtues? Will we practice these virtues or not? Truly, these virtues have an effect on our hearts. For example, rather than just uttering a praise of God, such as *La ilaha illallah* ("There is no God but God"), we must actually feel it, understand it, embrace it, and live it.

The Prophet said, "Whoever said *La ilaha illallah* (none has the right to be worshipped but God) and has in his heart good (faith) equal to the weight of a barley grain, will be taken out of Hell. And whoever said: *La ilaha illallah* and has in his heart good (faith) equal to the weight of a wheat grain will be taken out of Hell. And whoever said *La ilaha illallah* (none has the right to be worshiped but God) and has in his heart good (faith) equal to the weight of an atom (or a small ant) will be taken out of Hell." (*Sahih Bukhari*, vol. 1, book 2, chapter 33, Hadith 44)

One of the functions of the heart is *ta'aqqul* (understanding). God gave us a heart to open the four doors of His treasure: knowledge, reason, patience, and contentment.

A narration from Anas bin Malik quotes the Holy Prophet who said: "The Prophet David asked God; 'Oh God! All the emperors possess treasure then where is Your treasure?' God-Almighty replied: 'I possess a treasure that is greater than and is more beautiful than the Celestial Kingdom. Its earth is enlightenment; its sky is belief; its sun is enthusiasm; its moon is love. Its stars are inspiration and attention towards Me; its clouds are reason; its rain is blessing; its fruits are obedience; and its yield is wisdom. My Treasure has four doors, the first one is the door of knowledge, the second one is the door of reason, the third one is the door of patience, and the fourth one is the door of contentment. Know that My Treasure is the heart of a believer.'" (*Bihar al-Anwar*, vol. 70, p. 59)

To guide us toward these four doors and to self-actualize in their virtues, we should constantly repeat the following verse from the Qur'an, for it is one that has been bestowed upon those of Ahl al-Bayt who are endowed and well-rooted in knowledge and wisdom (*Raasikhoona fil ilm*).

(*They pray*) "Our Lord! Let not our hearts deviate now after You have guided us, but grant us mercy from Your

Own Presence; for You are the Grantor of bounties without measure." (Qur'an 3:8)

Islam guides and explains how to put these and other virtues of the pure heart into practice.

Chapter 8

Islamic Practices of the Pure Heart

The Islamic practices of the pure heart (*qalbun saleem*) are many, some of which are empathy (*atifah*), patience (*sabr*), ethics (*akhlaq*), and comfort (*salwan*).

Islamic Practices of *Qalbun Saleem*

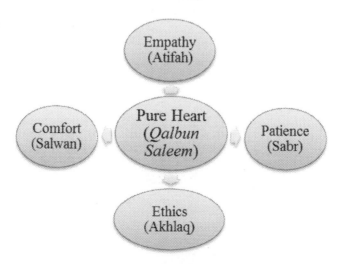

Empathy is identification with and understanding of another's situation, feelings, and motives. It is being aware of, being sensitive to, and experiencing the emotions and thoughts of others. Empathy may be tacit in that we feel what others feel without oral communication. It is synonymous with compassion, compatibility, congeniality, responsiveness, warmth, and understanding. Empathy derives from the pure heart (*qalbun saleem*).

It is the pure heart (*qalbun saleem*) that arouses our empathy. For example, empathy is an emotional intelligence of shared understanding in which each person assumes the other's perspective and cultural values as much as possible. Here, empathy requires mutual respect and goodwill between people to have an understanding for another person's beliefs and values. Preconceived ideas, stereotyped notions, and personal biases and prejudices are factors that make it difficult to achieve a shared understanding of another's feelings or emotions. For example, if we hold to the stereotype of a particular ethnic group as being "lazy," it will be difficult to empathize with homeless people from that ethnic group.

We regard empathy as a value the family engenders and strengthens to be cultivated at home. Yet we see vast evidence of its absence in children and adults. Ironically enough, a number of parents are without much empathy for their children, and vice versa. What really matters is that empathy can be taught, and it should be taught very early in life, at home and at school. It is not a matter of family values; it is a matter of society and civilization. There needs to be connectivity in the family, the school, and the society. Empathy can save a family; it can save lives.

The pure heart brings about genuine empathy. The connection between *qalbun saleem* and empathy is that of caring; caring, however, must be tempered with judgment and justice. Prophet Muhammad emphasized the importance of empathy with regard to feeling for others.

> Now has come to you a Messenger (*Muhammad*) from amongst yourselves; it grieves him that you should perish: he is ardently anxious over you: to the believers he is most kind and merciful. (Qur'an 9:128)

Empathy, discernment, and strength of character all rest within the pure heart. Empathy for others starts with the same point. We cannot truly feel the pain or the joy or the emotion of another (interpersonal) until we are able to feel the same thing in ourselves (intrapersonal). Do we acknowledge our own pain? Can we feel our own joy? Real empathy lies in simply finding the same place within us that the other person is experiencing. We might not have had exactly the same experience, but we've known the sadness of loss, or the anger of feeling cheated, or the sense of righteousness at injustice.

Empathy rests in the heart of *qalbun saleem*. Achieving empathy requires a great deal of diligence and thoughtfulness. It is difficult to have empathy when we are upset, angry, disappointed, or frustrated with another person. In such situations, our negative feelings will often serve as a roadblock, not permitting us to see the world through the eyes of the person with whom we are upset. We must learn to replace judgment with empathy, and ignorance with understanding.

The essence of patience (*sabr*) is when people restrain themselves from committing evil, obey God's orders by holding their hearts firm, and refrain from complaining about anything bad that happens to them. The best example of *sabr* is when people who are faced with calamity and adversity hold steadfast in their *sabr* and place their trust in God. Faith (*iman*) leads to patience (*sabr*), and patience leads back to faith. The linkage between faith and patience is the pure heart (*qalbun saleem*). *Sabr* has many attributes, such as patience and endurance. Imam Ali ibn Abi Talib said,

> Practice endurance (*sabr*): it is to faith what the head is
> to the body. There is no good in a body without a head,
> or in faith without endurance.

A body is useless without a head, since the brain is the chief mechanism for sustaining life. Likewise, faith is useless without endurance (*sabr*), since belief must be sustainable throughout one's entire life. Faith by itself is idealistic; with endurance it becomes realistic and actionable. Being steadfast in prayer, for example, guides the pious to the straight path (sirat al-mustaqim). God guides us to the straight path and overlooks our shortcomings. When we turn to God for guidance, we are protected from those who are deceived by complacency and materialistic gains of this world. Sabr has its roots in a deep-seated faith within the pure heart (qalbun saleem).

Patience (sabr) wins the pleasure of God. There is a constant need to be patient, whether in good times or in bad times. For example, assume that you are encircled by calamities, and your life, honor, and good name are in such peril—with no means of comfort available—that even visions, dreams, and revelations are suspended by God as a trial, and you are left helpless among terrible dangers. At such time, you should not lose heart or retreat like a coward or let your faithfulness be put in doubt in the least. Do not let your sincerity and perseverance be weakened. This is the patience (sabr) that leads to the devotion of God and secures the pure heart (qalbun saleem).

> And obey you God and his Apostle (Muhammad) and quarrel you not, for then you will be weakened in heart and will depart your power, and be patient; verily God is with the patient ones. (Qur'an 8:46)

Sabr becomes one of the most important aspects in our daily lives. It transcends what we call taqwah (consciousness of God). Thereafter, everything we do is kurbatan illallah; that is, to become nearer to God. Sabr is also known as miftah al-faraj (key to relief), and that key lies within the pure heart (qalbun saleem). It should be realized that in times of misfortune and hardship, God causes a light to descend upon the pure heart (qalbun saleem) of those He loves by strengthening them with great serenity. A true believer moves forward under misfortunes and submits completely to the will of God.

When we come to learn and understand the balance between sabr (patience) and qalbun saleem (pure heart), we gain an entirely new perspective about ourselves. One of the ways we can achieve this balance within the tranquil soul is by developing our Islamic personality. This personality makes us believers cherish our human dignity and prestige and accept our responsibilities as Muslims. And there's no better example of the Islamic personality than Prophet Muhammad, who said, "My religion is based on cleanliness." Cleanliness here does not just refer to our daily washing and cleansing of our bodies. There is a higher meaning, a meaning that attaches itself to the inner purity of the soul. We must cleanse our thoughts and nourish the pure heart (*qalbun saleem*) in order to attain ultimate and final perfection.

Ethics are moral principles that govern a person's behavior. Ethics are standards of right and wrong that prescribe what we ought to do. It also means to constantly examine our standards as to ensure they are reasonable. By studying our own moral beliefs and conduct, we can hold to ethical standards that are fermented within the pure heart (*qalbun saleem*).

Ethics (*akhlaq*) is the basis of the health or disease of the pure heart (*qalbun saleem*). The cultivation of *qalbun saleem* is an integral part of the ethical pursuit to purify the self, a tranquil inner self that is devoted to God. Immorality is due to diseases of the tranquil heart. Lack of morals causes destruction of the tranquil heart. When the tranquil heart does good things, it does so by using action nerves that emanate from the brain to the organs. Hence, ethics is the desire to do good things that originate from the tranquil heart. Moreover, ethics is having an innate sense of right and wrong and acting accordingly.

> O' mankind! We created you from a single (*pair*) of a male and a female, and made you into nations and tribes, that you may know each other (*not that you may despise each other*). Verily, the most honored of you with God is (*he who is*) the most righteous of you. And God has full knowledge and is well acquainted (*with all things*). (Qur'an 49:13)

Ethical practices have always been a crucial factor, particularly when integrity is compromised. Ethical standards are a direct reflection of our values. Questions dealing with trust, care, and excellence are ethical characteristics of sound leadership. Islam teaches us a code of ethics. We must espouse admirable traits in life by being friendly, sociable, and kind. Another important trait is that of justice and the capacity to defend our own rights. Hence, righteousness is rooted in the purity of *qalbun saleem*.

Ethical values are the foundation of Islam, as they afford to a pure heart (*qalbun saleem*) and to an exalted mind that conforms our wills to the will of God. Ethical values are the highest among all natural values. Ethical values grow out of conscious and free attitudes. The capacity to grasp ethical values, to affirm them, and to respond to them is the very nature of *qalbun saleem*. Since Islam encompasses all aspects of life and ethics, becoming aware and remembering God is the panacea to a tranquil and pure heart (*qalbun saleem*).

God provides us with tranquility. With a peaceful heart, tranquility becomes the foundation for comfort (*salwan*). Comfort is a practice we use often in our daily lives. To practice comfort independent of patience (*sabr*) renders its meaning and effectiveness to mediocrity. When combining it with *sabr*, however, we now have a fuller meaning and understanding. For example, to comfort (*salwan*) someone in her time of bereavement without patience (*sabr*) falls far short of being effective. However, to empathize—that is, to feel what the bereaved feels—and then to comfort her has much more effect and meaning. It places you in the position of the bereaved, as if you had suffered the loss as well. This is where *qalbun saleem* (pure heart) reaches its highest point.

> Verily, with (*every*) difficulty (*there*) is ease. Verily, with (*every*) difficulty (*there*) is ease. (Qur'an 94:5–6)

One of the most difficult aspects of our lives is when we fall victim to an emotion (*enfial*) that is out of control. The panacea for controlling our emotions is to comfort (*salwan*) both our inner selves and outer selves. A pure heart is a heart that has warmth and comfort that will make others feel cared for and in safe hands. Our minds give us our thoughts and ideas, but the pure heart makes the mind feel comfortable and loving.

As we go through life, we constantly seek comfort (*salwan*). We discover comfort by putting our trust and reliance in God. Life can be a painful journey, and finding comfort is not recognized unless we seek it, understand it, and embrace it. We cannot be comforted unless we know why we are being comforted. We must constantly remember (*dhikr*) God and find comfort in the purity of our hearts. It is God who enables our hearts to be pure, provided we make every effort to reach God and submit to His mercy and grace. There are many characteristics of the pure heart that enable us to understand its true meaning and significance in our daily lives.

Chapter 9

Characteristics of the Pure Heart

According to the Qur'an, the heart is a cognitive tool. Basically, the addressee of the main messages of the Qur'an is the heart. These messages are only heard from the heart, as ears are unable to hear them. Imam Ja'far as-Sadiq has said, "All things have heart and the heart of Qur'an is Surah Yaseen (*Bihar al-Anwar*, vol. 89, p. 288). The reason that Surah Yaseen is the heart of the Qur'an is because it contains all pillars of Islam; for example, the branches of faith (*Furu' al-Din*), such as the belief in God, belief in the prophets, and the belief in the hereafter, as well as the belief in the unity of God, the justice of God, the angels, the Imamat, and the books of God. Accordingly, as instruments of understanding, these messages and beliefs are absorbed and embodied within the characteristics of the pure heart (*qalbun saleem*) illustrated below:

Characteristics of the Pure Heart (*Qalbun Saleem*)

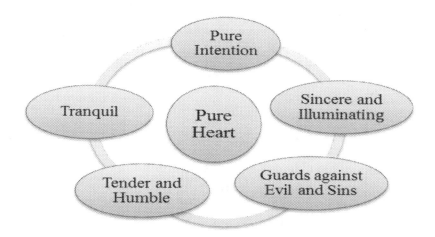

Pure Intention: Intention (*niyyah*) relative to our motives should always be in the direction of satisfaction and approval of God. As a consequence, God evaluates our deeds according to the intentions behind them. All the good deeds will become useless if the intention is corrupt. Intention is located in the heart.

> God will not call you to account for thoughtlessness in your oaths, but for the intention in your hearts; and He is Oft-Forgiving, Most Forbearing. (Qur'an 2:225)

If the heart is at the point of unrest, then the intention will be impure. The strength of our emotional intelligence brings about a strong intention. Intention requires energy to bring it into concentration.

We begin each day by making our intention to remember God. This intention puts us in the proper frame of mind. We make our intention to pray and perform the proper ablution, which not only cleans us from any physical impurities but also helps clear our hearts and minds from our daily stresses as part of our mental preparation for prayer. This quiets our thoughts and focuses our energy on God and away from external interferences or distractions.

Prophet Muhammad said: "No part of the salat (*prayer*) is yours except that part which you perform with an attentive heart." (*Bihar al-Anwar*, vol. 81, "Book of as-Salat," chapter 16, Hadith 59, p. 260)

Our actions are judged by our intentions. God will judge our actions based on the intentions behind those actions. The reward for our actions is according to our good intentions, and the punishment for our actions is according to our evil intention. We cannot gain anything from our actions except what is intended. So if the intention is good, the reward is good. If the intention is evil, the result is evil. If the action is sincere and incorrect, then it is not accepted. The action is only accepted when it is both sincere and correct. The action is sincere when it's done for the sake of God and correct when it's done according to the teachings of Islam. Hence, our actions are valued by the intentions we hold and the consciousness of the importance of doing them. In the words of Imam Ali ibn Abi Talib, "Pure intention is the ideal end and final aim" (*Nahjul Balagha*).

Sincere and Illuminating: If we work sincerely for the sake of God, God will compensate our sincerity (*ikhlas*) in a manner beyond our expectations. Imam Ali ibn Abi Talib reminds us:

> Sincerity is righteousness ... all efforts are naught except that which is sincerity ... the acceptance and exaltation of deeds depends on sincerity ... he who is sincere (*in his work*) shall realize his aspirations ... and when sincerity enters the heart, it is accompanied by glow and perspicacity." (*Nahjul Balagha*)

As sincere people, we set ourselves at God's disposal, make our hearts the sanctuary of this love, and allow divine motives to guide all our actions and behavior. In doing so, we attain honor and nobility.

What God seeks from us is the sincerity in our hearts. Sincerity toward God is the best type of sincerity. To be sincere in the heart, we have to be deeply devoted to God. And God knows what is in our hearts. If we are sincere with faith, belief, intention, obedience, morals and manners in our hearts, then God will reward us with His blessings. Sincerity is the pearl of the heart, collected from the depths of intention. Sincerity of heart means we act genuinely, honestly, solemnly, and passionately. It means we act without pretext or self-deception. Sincerity from the heart can touch the hearts of others. To fill our hearts with sincerity, we must empty them of impurities, such as corruption, dishonesty, negligence, and deceit. The sincere heart illuminates with strength and inspiration. It illuminates with wisdom. A grateful heart illuminates the straight path (*sirat al mustaqim*).

Guards against Evil and Sins: Guarding against a rebellious spirit and cultivating a spirit of submissive obedience to God is the first step toward guarding the heart. Guarding against a complaining spirit and cultivating a spirit of gratitude and trust is the second step toward guarding the heart. Avoiding anger, pride, and temptation is also a critical element of guarding the heart. In addition, we must guard our hearts in prayer, knowledge, wisdom, speech, perceptions, thoughts, and actions. The pure heart (*qalbun saleem*) guards against impure thoughts, vile affections, and desires that are instigated by Satan.

At the time of birth, the heart is pure and unblemished. Whenever an evil deed is committed, that evil deed marks a stain or rust on the heart. In order to remove that stain or rust, we must seek God's forgiveness and repent. Otherwise, the stain deepens and spreads more and more until the heart is sealed. Sins darken the heart with black spots. Any increase in sinning will only increase the black spots. The best way to guard the heart against evil and sins is to seal the windows of the heart with prayers, set a strong guard against outward senses, and inspect the heart daily. *Al-Kafi* divides the hearts into three divisions.

Divisions of the Heart

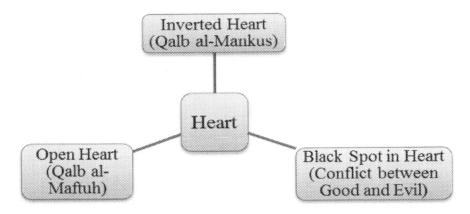

In the heart (*qalb al-mankus*), there is no good. This is the heart of an unbeliever. In the heart wherein there is a black spot, there is a conflict between good and evil, each of which seeks to overcome the other. In the open heart (*qalb al-maftuh*), there are lamps whose lights will not go out until the Day of Resurrection. This is the heart of the believer (*Al-Kafi*, vol. 2, p. 422, "Kitab al-Iman wa al-Kufr," "Bab Zulmah Qalb al-Munafiq," Hadith 3). When the irrational and rebellious heart becomes upright and righteous, it walks openly with God, as it rejoices in cleansing itself of sins and seeking His forgiveness. Furthermore, this steadfast and truthful heart is one of understanding, joy and happiness.

Tender and Humble: Islam mandates that we cultivate, nurture, and maintain our hearts with tender loving care. Having a tender heart is key to having a pure heart (*qalbun saleem*). One important act of those with tender hearts is to feed the needy and take care of the needs of orphans. Humility is the bedrock that opens the window of tenderness and softness in the heart so as to perform good deeds. It is the tender and humble heart that is faithful. One with a tender heart is sensitive to others, wants the best for them, rejoices when they rejoice, and mourns when they mourn. Those who have tender hearts are compassionate, loving, and focused on people. They are also trustworthy.

To maintain a tender heart is to value highly that tender heart.

Nor was Abraham's seeking forgiveness for his father otherwise than due to a promise which he had made unto him; but when it became clear unto him that he was an enemy unto God, he declared himself clear of him; verily Abraham was very tender-hearted, forbearing. (Qur'an 9:114)

To sustain that high value we must daily maintain our remembrance of God. To keep a tender heart we must extend our gratitude to God, along with our remembrance of Him. We must continually challenge ourselves to perform righteous deeds and utilize the gifts God has given us, rather than focus on the problems, disappointments, and difficulties of life. Tender and humble hearts are ever forgiving, as it makes us responsive to God.

Tranquil: The remembrance of God provides tranquility to the hearts. The only path to outer peace is awareness of the tranquil depths of inner peace, and the only source of such inner peace is God. Inner peace derives from the tranquil self that has overcome its lower aspects. This tranquil self is known as *nafs al-mutma'innah*, which is to be content with God. We are content with whatever God is content with. The tranquil self has reached a state of serenity, which means that it protects the self against committing sin and also from desiring sin. Thus, the tranquil self only desires good things. A tranquil heart is life to the body and free from envy. The tranquil heart is calm and confident. To cultivate the tranquil heart is to be in constant remembrance of God, to make prayer a priority, and to trust God with our circumstances in life. To cultivate the tranquil heart is to free it of the sins that disturb and disrupt it with its blemishes and black spots. When God sends the tranquility to the hearts of believers, they will not be tempted to deviate from the straight path:

He (*God*) it is who sent down tranquility into the hearts
of the faithful that theymight add further faith to their
faith. (Qur'an 48:4)

As will be detailed in the next chapter, the pure heart can be discussed
from the standpoint of various categories: types, kinds, and descriptions.

Chapter 10

Categories of the Pure Heart

It may be said that the heart is the king of the body. As such, all the components of the body are immobile unless the heart wants and intends to spark them. For example, the deeds or functions of the heart ignite the limbs of the body to become mobile. Whether the heart performs good deeds or bad deeds, it is the deciding entity of an individual's righteousness or corruption.

> Abu Thaalaba said: The Messenger of God said: "Righteousness is what achieves tranquility to one's soul and peace to one's heart, while sin disturbs the soul and the heart, even though numerous people should license you (*to do it*)." (*Al-Musnad Ahmad bin Hanbal*)

Since the heart reigns supreme, it is essential that the righteous person pay close attention to making it sound and upright. Satan, however, insidiously works to whisper evil thoughts into the heart to lure it to transgress by committing evil and sin. The only escape for the infected heart is to remember and rely on God for its cure. Let us examine the three types of heart: sound (*saleem*), diseased (*mareedh*), and dead (*mayyit*).

Types of the Heart (*Qalb*)

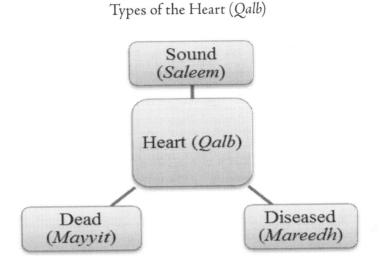

Sound Heart: The sound heart is the pure heart (*qalbun saleem*) that loves only those things that God loves and hates that which God hates. The sound heart is healthy and pure because it is free from any desires that oppose the commands of God and from any doubt that contradicts what God reveals. The sound heart submits completely and relies on God alone (Olatoye 2013). A servant with a healthy heart must dedicate it to its journey's end and not base his or her actions and speech on those of any other person, except God's messenger, Prophet Muhammad (Al-Hanbali 2015). The healthy, sound heart contains no impediment that prevents it from accepting the truth, loving it, and giving it preference, other than it's coming to know of it. Therefore, its recognition of the truth is correct, and it is complete with respect to its submission and acceptance of it (Shafi 2011). The sound heart is likened to the tranquil and serene heart (*nafs al-mutma'innah*).

> The day when will avail not wealth or sons, save him who comes unto God with a heart submissive. (Qur'an 26:88–89)

The sound heart is the tranquil soul of the virtuous believer that will return to God. This is the stage when the soul of a person being delivered from all weaknesses is filled with spiritual powers and establishes a relationship with God. Here, his patience (*sabr*) is achieved with complete success (Turfe 1996). Therefore, the one whose heart is described as *saleem* is such because it is flanked by both truth and security, which are constant protectors of the heart. Hence, the actions of the truthful and secure heart are purely to serve God.

Diseased Heart: The diseased heart is between the sound heart and the dead heart. It has some amount of life, but it is also defective. It contains love of God and faith in Him, but at the same time, it harbors a love of vain desires and the material world. It continuously wavers between the conditions of safety and destruction, and eventually it becomes a dead heart, if efforts are not made to purify it (Olatoye 2013). The diseased heart has life in it as well as illness. The former sustains it at one moment, the latter at another, and it follows whichever one of the two manages to dominate it. It is full of self-admiration, which can lead to its own destruction. It listens to two callers: one calling it to God and His prophet, Muhammad, and the other calling it to the fleeting pleasures of this world (Al-Hanbali 2015). When disease predominates in the heart, it joins the ranks of the dead and harsh hearts, but if its soundness predominates, it joins the ranks of the truthful and secure hearts (Shafi 2011).

> In their heart is a disease, and God increases their disease, for them is a painful chastisement, because of the lie they were saying. (Qur'an 2:10)

The diseased or sick heart is likened to the reproachful soul (*nafs al-lawwamah*). This is the soul that constantly upbraids itself in the quest for goodness. It is known as the reproving self or self-reproaching spirit. It reproves man on vice and is not reconciled to man's submitting to his natural desires. It desires that man should be in a good state and should practice good morals. As it reproves every vicious movement, it is called the reproving self. Here, man strives to achieve good but falls short of sustaining it. The self seeks to comprehend within itself high moral qualities and is disgusted with disobedience but cannot achieve complete success (Turfe 1996).

> Imam Ali said, "Surely want is a trial, and having sickness of the body is more difficult to bear than indigence, and having a sickness of the heart is more difficult to bear than having a sickness of the body. Surely, being very wealthy is a blessing, and having a healthy body is better than being very wealthy, and having awe of God in your heart is better than having a healthy body." (Nahjul Balagha)

Dead Heart: The dead heart is the direct opposite of the sound heart, as it has no life.

> Dead (*they are*), not living, and they perceive not when they will be raised. (Qur'an 16:21)

The dead heart neither recognizes its Lord nor worships Him. Hence, it is ignorant of its Creator. It follows its whims and desires and is immersed in worldly pleasures. It also engages in acts that it loves, regardless of whether God loves those acts or not. The dead heart is devoid of faith and devoid of all good. With such an unenlightened heart, Satan relaxes his whisperings, for he has already taken residence in this heart, a territory for him to rule as he pleases, for he has complete control (Olatoye 2013). The dead, harsh, and dry heart does not accept the truth nor submit to it (Shafi 2011).

Lust guides the dead heart. Its whims are its *imam* (leader). Its crude impulses are its impetus. It is drunk with its own fancies and its love for hasty, fleeting pleasures (Al-Hanbali 2015). This type of heart is similar to the evil soul (*nafs al-ammarah*). The mind of the individual is ever ready to incite to evil. This means that the human self urges the individual toward undesirable and evil ways, as it is opposed to the individual's attainment of moral perfection (Turfe 1996). Toward this end, the dead heart fulfills its hunger for worldly desires and does not care if God is pleased or displeased.

> Imam Ali replied, "There are four things that make the heart die: wrong action followed by wrong action, playing around with foolish people, spending a lot of time with women, and sitting with the dead." Then Imam Ali was asked: 'And who are the dead, O Commander of the believers?' He replied: "Every slave who follows his desires." (*Nahjul Balagha*)

Following is a comparison of selected characteristics of each of three types of hearts.

Selected Characteristics of the Types of Hearts

Sound Heart	Diseased Heart	Dead Heart
• Cleansed from evil and impurities	• Envious and abusive	• Doesn't know God
• Serves and remembers God	• Craves lust	• Doesn't worship God
• Moral excellence in conduct	• Craves material pleasures	• Lacks self-restraint and piety
• Performs righteous deeds	• Self-praise	• Clings to desires
• Constant in prayers	• Commits sin upon sin	• Loves material world

According to Hudhayfah ibn al-Yaman, a close companion of Prophet Muhammad, there are four kinds of hearts. The first heart is one that is untainted. This pure heart has a lantern that shines. This is the heart of a believer. The second kind of heart is wrapped up. This is the heart of a disbeliever. The third kind of heart is the one that is relapsed. This is the heart of a hypocrite. He knows the truth, but then he denies it. He sees the truth, but he closes his eyes. The fourth kind of heart is the one that is stretched out on two bodies: body of faith and body of hypocrisy. This kind of heart is with whichever body dominates it (Al-Jawziyyah 2012).

Kinds of Hearts

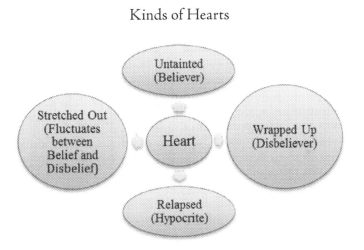

Ibn Qayyim Al-Jawziyyah explained the meaning of the four kinds of hearts hypothesized by Hudhayfah ibn al-Yaman. The untainted heart is rid of everything other than God and Prophet Muhammad. It is free and safe from falsehood. The lantern that shines is the lamp of faith. It is free from false doubts that resemble the truth and desires that lead astray. Due to the heart being in this state, it has obtained a lantern that illuminates it and sends out light. This light is the radiance of knowledge and faith.

The wrapped-up heart is the heart of a *kafir* (disbeliever). The disbeliever's heart is covered in its wrapping and cloak. Since the heart is covered tightly, the light of *iman* (faith) and knowledge cannot reach it.

The relapsed heart means that God has caused the hypocrites to suffer a relapse and go back to falsehood. They were in this falsehood because of the dishonesty in their deeds. The relapsed heart is the most wicked kind of heart. It believes that falsehood and lies are true. Poeple with this kind of heart in their chests fight falsely against the truth.

The stretched-out heart is stretched between two bodies—faith and hypocrisy. This kind of heart doesn't have *iman* (faith) firmly established in it. Therefore, its light doesn't shine. It doesn't hold the absolute truth in it. However, it has some truth and some falsehood inside. Hence, sometimes disbelief is stronger than belief inside of it and vice versa. Whichever one of these two elements is the strongest in the heart, this is the one it turns to at that time (Al-Jawziyyah 2012).

In the Qur'an, four words describe the heart: *qalb* (proper heart), *fuaad* (kindling or inner heart), *sadr* (breast or chest), and *lubb* (pure intellect). These descriptions or stations of the heart are arranged in concentric spheres, the breast (*sadr*) being the outermost sphere, followed on the inside by the proper heart (*qalb*), the inner heart (*fuaad*), and the pure intellect (*lubb*). The proper heart (*qalb*) is higher and purer than the chest or breast (*sadr*); and the inner heart (*fuaad*) is higher and purer than the proper heart. The heart's core or pure intellect (*lubb*) is higher and purer than the inner heart.

Descriptions of the Heart

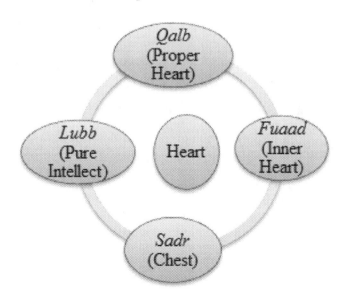

Fuaad, the kindling or inner heart is mentioned in the Qur'an (6:113, 11:120, 14:37, 14:43, 16:78, 17:36, 25:32, 28:10, 53:11). It is the heart inflamed with emotion, such as happiness or sadness, anger or tranquility, love or hate. It has also been called the emotional cover around the *qalb* (proper heart), which indicates that *fuaad* does not get deep into the heart but remains at its outer boundary. However, scholars have differed on this interpretation, as some are of the opinion that *fuaad* enters deep into the heart in that it is the place where witnessing takes place and the light of knowing God is kindled. Here is where the blaming self (*nafs al-lawwamah*) resides. When the mother of Prophet Moses put her newborn baby into the Nile River, her heart was inflamed with burning emotion. She was distraught with having to give up her son to ensure his safety. However, God strengthened her heart, as she put her trust and reliance in God.

> And the heart of the mother of Moses became tranquilled;
> she was about to disclose it had we not strengthened
> her heart so that she might be of the believers (*in Our
> promise*). (Qur'an 28:10)

Sadr (chest) is another description of the heart that is used when God is alluding to "expanding the breast" or outer layers of the heart. *Sadr* is mentioned in the Qur'an (3:154, 6:125, 7:2, 7:43, 11:5, 11:12, 15:97, 16:106, 20:25, 26:13, 39:22, 40:56, 94:1, 114:5). Influences on the heart are not in its inner layers but at the outer layers. As to the inner layers of the heart, the individual is held responsible if the heart is pure or impure. Here, the self exhorts to evil (*nafs al-ammarah*). *Sadr* is also a place where secrets and motives are kept, where one's ego takes control, and where Satan whispers into the heart.

> Who (*Satan*) whispers into the breasts (hearts) of the
> people, (*be he*) from among the Jinn and the men? (Qur'an
> 114:5–6)

Lubb is a description of the heart that is referred to as the pure intellect. The *lubb* is the pure intellect that is free from inner stains and doubt. *Lubb* or *albaab* (those of understanding) is mentioned in the Qur'an (2:179, 2:197, 2:269, 3:7, 3:190, 5:100, 12:111, 13:19, 14:52, 21:79, 38:29, 38:43, 39:9, 39:18, 39:21, 40:54, 65:10). When God refers to *iman* (faith) and the diseases of the heart, He uses the word *lubb*, which transforms into *qalbun saleem* (pure heart). The heart can accept or reject immoral acts such as materialism, but once the heart absorbs them, it can reach all the way to the core of the heart (*lubb*), thereby damaging it, resulting in a major setback for *qalbun saleem*. Removing stains from *qalbun saleem* is very difficult and painful and requires constant cleansing, like squeezing a sponge to remove them. The prescription for protecting the pure heart (*qalbun saleem*) is to be in constant remembrance (*dhikr*) of God. It is *dhikr* that provides layers of protection around the pure heart (*qalbun saleem*).

The components of the spiritual self are the *aql* (intellect), *nafs* (desire), and *lubb* (heart).

Components of the Spiritual Self

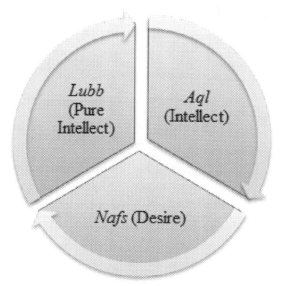

While every *lubb* is an intellect, not every intellect (*aql*) reaches the level of a *lubb*. The desire (*nafs*) determines whether or not the intellect reaches the *lubb*. Intellect (*aql*) trains and controls our desires. Intellect must rule over desire in order to reach the peaceful heart of *lubb*. The healthy and sound heart reaches the state of *lubb* because it is free from any desires that oppose the commands of God and from any doubt that contradicts what God reveals. On the other hand, if the desires are absorbed in material pleasures, then the heart is the direct opposite of the healthy heart, as it has no life—it is, in fact, a dead heart (*qalbu'l mayyit*).

God often uses the term *Ulul-Albaab*, the people of hearts, to refer to those intellectual believers who are in touch with the innermost core that recognizes the signs of God and understands the truth, free from the unrestrained emotions of *fuaad* and beyond the irresolute indecisiveness of the heart. *Lubb* is truly the heart of hearts (Misra 2009). Here is where the peaceful spiritual self (*nafs al-mutma'innah*) resides. This is also where the pure intellect (*lubb*) of the Infallible Imams of Ahl al-Bayt resides.

> He grants wisdom to whomsoever He wills, and he who has been granted wisdom has been given abundant good; and none shall mind it save those endowed with the cores (*lubb*) of wisdom. (Qur'an 2:269)

The main elements of the heart can be summarized in the following table:

Element	Qalb	Fuaad	Sadr	Lubb
Station	Proper Heart	Inner Heart	Breast (Chest)	Intellect
Kind of Heart	Normal	Kindled	Relapsed	Pure
Attribute	Faithful	Gnostic	Egoistic	Unifier
Function of Heart	Turns Over	Burns/ Flames	Hidden Secrets/ Motives	Sinless
Expectation	Interior Knowledge of Reality	Vision of Reality	Distorted Knowledge	God's Grace/ Bounty
Soul/Self	Inspired	Reproving/ Blaming	Evil	Serene/ Peaceful
Outcome	Heart Expands and Contracts	Inflamed with Emotions	Expanding the Breast (Outer Layers of Heart)	Divine Guidance
Faith	Believer	Believer	Disbeliever	Pious
Belief	Knows God	Knows God	Inspired by Satan	God Fearing

There are many signs, benefits, and achievements of the pure heart (*qalbun saleem*). We reflect on each of these in order to reflect on maintaining and sustaining the purity of the heart.

Qalbun Saleem

Signs, Benefits, and Achievements of *Qalbun Saleem*

Signs	Benefits	Achievements
✦ Remembers God	✦ Contentment and inner peace	✦ Spiritual enlightenment
✦ Loves for the sake of God	✦ Steadfastness in practicing Islam and obeying God	✦ Control consciousness via meditation
✦ Gives for the sake of God	✦ Success in this life and the hereafter	✦ Morally and intellectually sound
✦ Forbids for the sake of God	✦ Focused and avoids distractions	✦ Self-purification

Signs are a reflection of the purpose of our existence. We often follow these signs or seek them. The best source of determining what these signs are is found in the Qur'an and the Hadiths. The signs of a pure heart (*qalbun saleem*) are many; for example, loves and hates what God loves and hates, gives only for the pleasure of God, and never misses an opportunity to worship God. One such sign is a repentant heart (*qalbun muneeb*), which is concerned with devotion and pleasure of God, immediately repenting once a sin is committed (Qur'an 50:33). Hence, repentance is the sign of a believer who asks God for forgiveness immediately after committing a flagrant violation of the soul and contamination of the pure heart. Not only does the person repent, but he or she also changes to establish a constant relationship with God. Repentant hearts always maintain respect for God by turning their attention to Him, humbles themselves before Him, and giving up their sensual and base desires. The Qur'an underscores the importance of these signs.

> Verily, in the creation of the heavens and the earth and the alteration of the night and the day, there are signs for men who possess wisdom. Those who remember God standing, and sitting and reclining on their sides and think (*seriously*) in the creation of the heaven and the earth; saying "O' Our Lord! Thou has not created (*all*) this in vain! Glory be to Thee! Save us then from the torment of the (*Hell*) fire." (Qur'an 3:190–191)

> And say thou, "All praise is God's. Soon will He show you His signs that you shall recognize them;" and thy Lord is not heedless of what all you do. (Qur'an 27:93)

> Yet was not enjoined on them but that they should worship God (*alone*) in perfect sincerity, in religion (*only*) unto Him, and that they give away the poor-rate, and that is the religion (*correct and*) strong. (Qur'an 98:5)

Other signs to reflect on are (1) moral excellence, (2) contentment, (3) firmness, (4) honesty, (5) forgiveness, (6) forbearance, and (7) generosity. These are the signs of the devoted and pure heart (*qalbun saleem*). We begin to understand that the whole universe, including all its beings, is a sign of God's power. The benefits of *qalbun saleem* are that we attain contentment and inner peace and are firm in our faith. The achievements of *qalbun saleem* are being in constant remembrance of God, as we spiritually purify the heart and cure its diseases.

AHL AL-BAYT

Chapter 11

Spirituality: Cures for the Diseases of the Pure Heart

If the heart controls the issues of life—attitudes, behaviors, ambitions, desires, and feelings—life's problems eventually are problems of the heart. In order to have a healthy body and mind, we need to bring into balance food and nutrition, fitness and exercise, and relaxation and stress management. With a positive attitude, we can motivate ourselves to improve our overall health and well-being. We are constantly seeking better ways to improve our health and lifestyles. The energy fields of the physical (body), emotional (heart), mental (mind), and spiritual (soul) can have an effect on the entire body's health system.

We need a reconnect to improve our health situation, and that reconnect is Islam. Some of the reasons we seek this reconnect are as follows:

+ physical sickness, surgery, disability
+ emotional despondency, hopelessness, sadness
+ mental lapse, disorientation, depression
+ spiritual decline, disenchantment, distrust

These health issues require immediate attention and help. Something is wrong. We can turn to Islam and its benefits to reconnect and energize our health. The following displays how Islam transforms, reconnects, and energizes health to bring about our overall well-being.

Energy Transformation
Islamic Health Reconnect

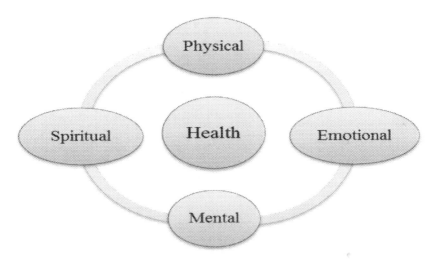

The benefits derived from an Islamic reconnect are manifold. Some of these are as follows:

- alleviates physical pain from trauma (praying)
- eliminates metabolic wastes in body (fasting)
- enriches emotional well-being (praying)
- manages stress (fasting)
- heightens mental awareness (praying)
- enhances piety and spirituality (fasting)

The heart is the place of courage and spirit, integrity, and commitment—the source of energy and deep feelings that call us to create, learn, cooperate, lead, and serve. When we have painful feelings, the heart is telling us we have unmet needs, or we are interpreting reality through a type of distorting filter. When we have positive feelings, the heart is telling us we are pointing in the right direction, toward fulfillment of our needs and toward truth.

> Fight them, that God may chastise them by your hands and put them to shame, and help you (*in victory*) over them and heal the (*injured*) breast (heart) of a believer people. And remove He the rage of the hearts. And God turns (*merciful*) unto whomsoever He pleases. (Qur'an 9:14–15)

According to DeLaune and Ladner, people throughout history have dealt with pain, illness, and healing in spiritual ways. Many people believe their spirituality helps promote healing, especially when medications and other treatments cannot provide a cure for their conditions. Health care professionals are entrusted with the holistic care of their clients. Spiritual care is a part of holistic care (DeLaune and Ladner 2006). Islam takes a holistic approach to health. Physical, emotional, mental, and spiritual health cannot be separated, as they are four parts that make a person completely healthy.

Energetic health, on a spiritual level, can close the gap between who we are and who we aspire to be. In the spiritual sense, there is a greater purpose in life. Widespread evidence shows that the interest in spirituality is not confined to individuals who attend religious centers or who are identified as being religious (Shea 2000). Spirituality is an integral part of the health and well-being of every individual. We see creation everywhere, and we marvel at the wonders of this creation. We know a greater force exists that connects everything together.

We are energetic beings, and it is the spiritual aspect of energy that reinforces the physical, emotional, and mental aspects of our health. If we lack worship, then our health is adversely impacted. Researchers have discovered a positive relationship between religion and physical health, and they have demonstrated that spiritual beliefs and practices are beneficial to health and can help reduce the risk of developing a number of serious illnesses (Ebersole and Hess 1997).

For our bodies and minds to be healthy, we need to lead lives of spirituality. Spiritual values need to be integrated into our lifestyles. The power of prayer and meditation brings all the energy forces of physical, emotional, mental, and spiritual in harmony with each other. Recent studies have shown a statistically significant relationship between religious involvement, better mental health, and greater social support. They have also found that almost 80 percent of those who are religious have significantly greater well-being, hope, and optimism than those who are less religious (Micozzi 2006).

Diseases of the Heart

While there are numerous emotional diseases of the heart, some are often referred to as the *seven deadly sins*, which dates back to the fourth century. At that time, struggle with sinful and evil thoughts or attitudes could only be overcome by the grace of God, which was received through practicing spiritual disciplines (Sinkewicz 2003). These seven deadly sins, or diseases of the heart, are pride, greed, gluttony, sloth, anger, envy, and lust (Jeffrey 1992). The seven corresponding cures are humility, generosity, temperance, diligence, patience, kindness, and purity (Webb 1965). There are many other diseases of the heart, such as egoism, hatred, jealousy, pessimism, and doubt.

> In their hearts is a disease, and God increases their disease, for them is a painful chastisement, because of the lie they were saying. (Qur'an 2:10)

Let us examine a few of these diseases with their corresponding cures.

Diseases of the Heart

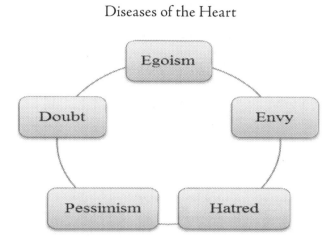

Egoism: From various dictionaries, we find many meanings of the term *ego*. Ego is the conscious mind and the consciousness of one's own identity. Egoism is the doctrine that the supreme end of human conduct is the perfection of happiness of the ego, or self, and that all virtues consist in the pursuit of self-interest. It is the habit of valuing everything only in reference to our personal interests. It is the ethical doctrine that morality has its foundations in self-interest. It is the ethical belief that self-interest is the just and proper motive for all human conduct. It is the excessive preoccupation with our own well-being and interests, usually accompanied by an inflated sense of self-importance. It is the tendency to evaluate everything in relation to our own interests; that is, self-centeredness.

Egotism is the habit or practice of thinking and talking about ourselves, or the spirit that leads to this practice; for example, self-exaltation. It is the tendency to think only about ourselves and to consider ourselves to be better and more important than other people. It is an exaggerated opinion of our own importance and an inflated feeling of pride in our superiority to others. It is the concept in which we are so possessed by the ego that we become convinced that we are the center of the universe.

Whether someone is egoistic or egotistic, he is morally depraved and suffers from false impressions of himself. This self-centeredness and self-absorption within himself immensely diminishes his chances of ever reaching moral fulfillment and self-respect. Keeping occupied with thoughts and actions of materialism, greed, being the center of attention, and conceit, he continues to fall deeper and deeper into a spiral pit from which he cannot escape. This obedience to his self further erodes his soul, as he commits every act of transgression, deception, and sedition in order to achieve his superiority or authority over others. In a nutshell, he begins to worship himself, thereby becoming totally impervious to spirituality and the common good.

> Have thou seen him who takes his vain (ego) inclinations
> for his god? Would thou then be a guardian over him?
> (Qur'an 25:43)

The person who is continually boasting about himself is someone whose self-worth is meaningless, and he feels the necessity to tap other avenues or sources to restore his self-esteem. This need for replenishment is vital, since the ego functions out of fear. The ego operates in such a way as to give the egotist a sense of loneliness and separation from the world. The egotist feels he is obliged to act the way he does, as no one really cares about him. This leads him to constantly seek approval in any way he can get it. His addiction to his inner self makes him even more anxious to not only seek approval from others but to demand it as well. The end result is that the egotist finds himself rejected by others. Still, the egotist revitalizes himself and seeks other means for acceptance, even if it means engaging in corruption and immoral acts to achieve it.

A Muslim fulfills his needs by devoting himself to spirituality and not to vanity and conceit. Spirituality helps mold his personality and sets him on the right track. Vanity and conceit severely limit the person's striving for self-worth, thereby resulting in humiliation and disgrace. With humility and self-sacrifice, he can recover his sense of worth and regain his spirituality, free of pride and complacency. There is no room for selfish ambition or vain conceit or self-delusions. Those who have the superior attitude that they are always right portray this kind of approach. They confront others to prove their point, and they must have the final say in all matters. Rather than recognizing their mistake, they keep on pressing forward against those who support truth. Egotists feel that those who oppose them are rivals. But the real rival is the rival within each of them.

With a lack of unity within himself, the egotist becomes weak, suffers from low morale, and consumes his energy focusing on trivial issues and problems. This, in turn, leads to personality clashes and enmity. The egotist is ignorant about his obligation to strive for unity within himself and within others. The love of this life and the propensity to control others are reasons for discord. To combat egotism, we must have a strong sense of solidarity and brotherhood, whereby we better understand one another and work toward the common good. We must cling to the *Rope of God* with every ounce of energy and determination to succeed (Turfe 2004).

Envy: Envy is a feeling of discontent or covetousness with regard to another's advantages, success, or possessions. It is often referred to as one of the seven deadly sins. Envy is a common sin and the perpetual tormenter of virtue. Envy is treacherous because it draws people to its venom. Envy renders its victims miserable and unhappy. Envy is associated with hypocrisy, hatred, and discord. Envy is like a vampire who feeds on others. Envy pollutes the heart.

> Many of the people of the scripture wish to turn you back to infidelity after you had believed, out of selfish envy on their part after the Truth had been manifested unto them; but forgive you and overlook you till God brings about His command. Verily, God is over all things Powerful. (Qur'an 2:109)

Envy is a complex and puzzling emotion. According to the Greek philosopher Aristotle, envy is pain at the good fortune of others. Envy is a frustrated desire turned destructive. In envy, the impulse to make contact with others becomes the impulse to destroy others. An envious person wants to destroy the morals and ethics of others. An envious person works to demoralize others so as to adversely impact their lives. Envy distorts and then insidiously works toward devouring the thoughts and views of others.

While jealousy is directed toward the possession of values, envy is directed toward the destruction of values. Envy works out of fear and resentment toward others. Survival for those who envy is fed by an insatiable diet of consuming the values of others. Ignorance breeds suspicion, and suspicion breeds envy, all of which are incompatible with the essential attitude of sympathy and love. In addition, greed also breeds envy and hate. Imitation is the result of envy. Many social structures are based on envy and imitation. One of the main causes of division in a society is envy and the craving for success; each is imitating the one above him. Envy spreads between Muslims, differentiating their hearts and making them hate one another. Envy transcends in to selfish transgression, which is one of the causes of disunity and division among Muslims.

The remedy for envy is love. Envy is born in hate and is cured in love. In Islam, the word envy is called *hasad*, which is the desire toward destruction of something good that belongs to someone else. *Hasad* is the most destructive and greatest obstacle toward establishing and cementing relationships between Muslims. Envy can be overcome by the spirituality of Muslims in the direction of cooperation, comfort, and confidence. Remember we are the members of the same *Ummah* (Muslim community). We can strive for unity in the community if we overcome ignorance, allay our fears and suspicions, and combat envy with love and respect for one another (Turfe 2004).

Hatred: Hatred is a pervasive emotion and sociopsychological problem. As defined in a dictionary, hatred takes on many forms. It is enmity, hostility, antagonism, animosity, rancor, antipathy, and animus. Enmity is hatred such as might be felt for an enemy. Hostility implies the clear expression of enmity. Antagonism is hostility that quickly results in active resistance, opposition, or contentiousness. Animosity often triggers bitter resentment or punitive action. Rancor suggests vengeful hatred and resentment. Antipathy is deep-seated aversion or repugnance.

Animus is distinctively personal, often based on one's prejudices or temperament.

How does hatred manifest itself in the human persona? People who are imbued with hatred feel that they have been unfairly treated, unjustly accused, or betrayed. Perhaps their honor was questioned, or their needs were never understood, or they never received recognition. As a result, they begin to hate and harbor the most extreme level of anger against those who hurt them. They become agitated and antagonistic toward others. In addition, they become inflamed, rude, and belligerent toward others. Reasons for this hatred against others may be that they feel that lies, cheating, rejection, and condemnation victimized them. They may feel that they were used and abused. Because of this enmity, those who hate are never fully content. Rather, they are bitter, hostile, sarcastic, embittered, paranoid, suspicious, and defensive. They are irrational in their behavior, as they feel there is no hope for tolerance; just despair and distrust. Hatred stems from the power of anger and destroys an individual's spiritual balance.

To overcome hatred, those who hate must be able to assess and analyze their own irrational behavior. They must identify how others react to them. When they evaluate the causes of their own hatred, is it a figment of their imagination, or is it real? Were they intentionally being mistreated or neglected? Or were they just wrapped up in their own egos?

There is much concern about hatred in the world. Is each diverse culture too myopic and autonomous to look outside itself at other cultures for workable insights and solutions? Are we so wrapped up in the evolution of technology and change that we are incapable of effectively dealing with hatred? Hatred has no single location, for it permeates throughout all aspects of national, ethnic, and religious spheres. And within these spheres, hatred often erupts into violence and war. Hatred is often nourished by ignorance. Ignorance breeds hatred, as it closes our eyes to what is actually happening. Ignorance isolates people from the rest of humanity. Lack of knowledge is the ultimate barrier. Ignorance enslaves and leads to the enslavement of others. At the core of the struggle with hatred and ignorance are issues of the lack of community involvement.

O' you who have believed! Take not intimates, other than your fellow believers. They will not fail to corrupt you; they wish what distresses you (*the most*); their spite (*hatred*) has already shown itself out of their mouths, but that which is concealed in their breasts (*hearts*) is greater still; indeed We have made clear the signs unto you, if you would understand. (Qur'an 3:118)

Here in America we are confronted with the disease of xenophobia, or fear and hatred of strangers and foreigners. It is fear of that which is different. It is fear that leads to hatred and a desire for control over those who are different. Xenophobia is based on ignorance. Ignorance breeds fear. Fear brings about intolerance. Intolerance gives rise to hatred. Unlike many other countries, most Americans speak only one language—English. In America, we find many people who are ignorant and naïve regarding other cultures and nations, and the foreign policy of the American government, at times, is representative of this unjust reality. For example, the American government's lack of a genuine even-handed policy in the Middle East has severely tarnished its credo of democracy and justice.

There is a lack of trust, partnership, and shared values among people within the same community. To be sure, reconciliation in resolving religious disputes, in resolving ethnic quarrels, and in resolving marital problems is a great challenge if brotherhood and solidarity are to be effective. Hatred, in all forms, not only offends the dignity of humankind but also is an offense against God. In overcoming hatred, Muslims must seek ways to foster the vitality and moral well-being of the society. Islam offers us the way to enlightenment. When hatred appears, Islam provides the solution to overcome this evil. Islam provides the necessary and trustworthy values, norms, motivations, and ideals, all grounded in an ultimate reality. To overcome hatred, we can extend a helping hand to one another by being compassionate and understanding. Above all, we must be forgiving, even of those who hate. We must overlook the mistakes of others as we learn how to forgive (Turfe 2004).

Pessimism: Pessimism is the tendency to emphasize or think of the bad part of a situation rather than the good part, or the feeling that bad things are more likely to happen than good things. Pessimists look at the worst side of a situation and take the opposing view in any positive conversation. Pessimists turn conversations into griping and complaining. They ridicule attempts to rectify a dysfunctional situation.

Pessimism is a dangerous spiritual illness. It is the cause of many losses, defects, and disappointments. Pessimism is a painful calamity that torments the human soul and leaves irreparable defects on an individual's personality that cannot be expunged. Why is there this erratic behavior on the part of pessimists? Pessimists feel they are isolated or abandoned as well as deceived, resentful, and uninvited. Pessimists lack friendly interaction with others because they are adamant and one-sided in their views. Other reasons for this erratic behavior on the part of pessimists may be due to tragic events in their lives. These tragic events can range from the loss of a family member to affliction with a permanent disability. They may be shameful of having done something wrong and are unable to seek atonement and forgiveness for their transgressions. When pessimists are continually reminded of their shortcomings, they become very resentful and seek revenge. When undergoing pain or annoyance, they tend to become overly responsive by exhibiting adverse emotional outbursts as they revolt against those they see as their enemies.

Pessimism inflicts anxiety and pain to its victims and ultimately denies them hope and optimism. The damaging effect of pessimism harms the body and corrodes the soul. Pessimists experience seclusion and distrust when interacting with others. How do people overcome pessimism? There needs to be a reassessment in their lives. They need to reassess their behavioral patterns with those with whom they interact. This requires recognition and identification of their deficient behaviors and attitudes as to how this negatively impacts them as well as others. They must rejuvenate their spirituality and reconnect with faith. The Qur'an clearly counts pessimism among the sins and evil deeds and cautions Muslims about thinking negatively of each other.

O' you who believe! Avoid such suspicion (*pessimism*), for verily suspicions (*in*) some (*cases*) is a sin, and spy you not, and let not some of you backbite the others. (Qur'an 49:12)

When Prophet Mohammad came on the scene, he was confronted with pessimism from every direction. During the pre-Islamic Age of Ignorance (*jahiliyah*), people were overly pessimistic, even to the point of being absorbed by superstitions. One example was the Islamic month of Safar. At the time of Prophet Mohammad, disbelievers strongly felt that month was taboo. As a result, marriage ceremonies, trade transactions, and endeavors in general were forbidden. Disbelievers actually felt that to engage in these activities during that month would inflict hardships and disasters upon them. When Prophet Mohammad appeared, he instilled within the community a sense of reliance on God.

Prophet Mohammad abhorred, with great distaste, any act of pessimism. All forms of pessimism are unacceptable in Islam. Prophet Mohammad exercised all possible endeavors in explaining the evils of pessimism. He made it unmistakable that we need to purify our hearts from thinking evil or being pessimistic. Social order and unity benefit from optimism, while decay and disintegration of the society are the consequences of pessimism (Turfe 2004).

Doubt: Another disease is doubt or suspicion. The Qur'an reminds us:

It is the Truth from thy Lord so be thou not of those who doubt. (Qur'an 2:147)

The Truth is from thy Lord; therefore, be not thou of those of the doubters. (Qur'an 3:60)

He it is Who created you of clay, then decreed the term (*of your life*); and the term determined is with Him and yet you doubt (*thereof*). (Qur'an 6:3)

Only they ask leave of thee (*to be exempt*) who believe
not in God and the Last   Day (*of Judgment*), and
their hearts are in doubt, hence in their doubt they are
tossed to and fro. (Qur'an 9:45)

Is in their heart any disease or do they doubt, or fear they
lest will unjustly deal with them God and His apostle?
Nay! They themselves are the unjust ones. (Qur'an 24:50)

Doubt erodes the very soul of man who becomes paralyzed with his
vital functions and spiritual faculties. According to Ayatullah Sayyid
Abdul Husayn Dastghaib Shirazi:

The sign of the soundness of a man's heart is that he
is sure and confident about the truth being correct
and falsehood being incorrect and is in the position of
knowledge and conviction, while the sign of the disease
of the heart with respect to understanding truth and
falsehood is that there is suspense and doubt regarding
the rightfulness of truth and the refutation of falsehood.
Indeed, the heart devoid of the recognition of truth and
the effulgence knowledge and belief is not worth being
called a human heart. He is ignorant of a pure life and
his life is inferior like that of animals. Doubt is a kind of
blindness. A blind man remains doubtful of those things
also which are just spread around him because he does
not see them. If a thing is proved true by wisdom, by
conscience and by rational argument, and   one still
doubts about it, then surely the eyes of his heart are
blind. He is deprived of the blessing of discernment.
Reason and Shariah command, and the paramount
responsibility of such a person is that he should try to
obtain the cure of his disease of doubt. (Shirazi 2015)

We experience life and ask many questions. Some of these questions may raise doubt or suspicion in our minds. The greatest disease is to doubt the existence of God. Doubt leads to disbelief in God. Imam Ali ibn Abi Talib reminds us, "He who purifies his heart from doubt is a believer." When we experience doubt, it is because of the lack of knowledge or the weakness of our faith. To overcome these doubts we must consult with Islamic scholars who have the knowledge and the requisite training to address such issues. We must reflect upon the words of God via the Qur'an, the teachings of Prophet Muhammad, and the Hadiths.

Part of the reason that people feel emptiness in their prayers is because they feel that by praying and fasting and supplicating, they are doing something to benefit God and that He should feel obliged to reimburse them for their efforts. Then, they desire certain outcomes that their limited insight feels is best for them, and if those do not occur, then God has not answered them, so they become despondent and doubtful. Perhaps the reward for their steadfast prayers and devotions for all these years since they became Muslims is that even through their difficult times of doubting the very One who gave them all of these blessings, He still enables them to worship Him and keeps them connected to Him, out of His love and divine concern for them (Misra 2010).

Questioning is not a disease, but being blinded by ego and falsehood is a disease. People argue about God and don't take God's words seriously. Even though God provides them with the means that erases any doubts, they continue to be steadfast in their ignorance. The cure for these suspicious and doubtful minds is to genuinely pursue the knowledge of the truth God has provided them. As such, they will be redeemed, increase their belief, and obliterate any doubts they have. However, only those who choose the path God has given them will pursue His guidance as they witness His proofs and signs. Bottom line is that they have to read the Qur'an and reflect on its verses with patience and a pure heart (qalbun saleem).

Chapter 12

Qur'an Promotes Healing
of the Pure Heart

The most effective prescription for treating psychological disorders that adversely impact the heart is the Qur'an, which is a guide and treatment that heals our mental attitudes and disciplines our minds. The Qur'an rehabilitates our well-being in order to improve the quality of our faith. It nourishes our souls and prepares us to be patient (*sabr*), which is the springboard toward contemplation (*fikr*), bringing us closer to the straight path (*sirat al mustaqim*) and remembrance (*dhikr*) of God. As a result, we improve our mental consciousness that energizes our Islamic personality.

Moreover, our mental consciousness will thereby reduce confusion, worry, stress, depression, and other psychological disorders. Throughout life, we are beset with myriad social and psychological problems that become more and more complex and difficult to solve. The Qur'an provides the means for preventive healing, constructive and rehabilitative aspects that will improve our Islamic personality. Furthermore, the Qur'an brings into focus the body, mind, soul, and heart that are at peace in Islam, even with our trials and tribulations.

Prayer is the *dhikr* (remembrance) of God.

> Therefore, remember Me, I will remember you, and be
> thankful to Me and (*be*) not ungrateful. (Qur'an 2:152)

In prayer, our consciousness makes us aware of God. It is a reminder that performing good deeds and avoiding sin brings us closer to God. We must make our verbal declaration of *dhikr*. Hence, recitation of the Qur'an, purification of the heart, and prayer invoke the remembrance of God. It has been said that the heart of the Qur'an is Surah Yasin.

> Imam Ja'far as-Sadiq said, "Indeed everything has a
> heart and the heart of Qur'an is Surah Yasin. Thus, one
> who recited it before the daybreaks will be protected
> and sustenance would be provided to him. And one
> who recites this before going to bed, God will make a
> thousand angels protect him from every Satan and every
> loss and if he dies that day, God will make him enter
> Paradise." (*Makarimul Akhlaq*, p. 364)

The Qur'an is referred to as the reminder (*dhikr*), and likewise, Sura Yasin, a chapter of the Qur'an, is also a reminder. When we become immersed in *dhikr*, every cell of our bodies repeats the *dhikr*. Once we invoke *dhikr*, then *dhikr* invokes us. It becomes part of our unconscious as it alters our mental, psychological, and physical bodies in positive ways. The effect of *dhikr* is more powerful than just an act of mental focusing. The end result of this process is that we are reprogrammed for God. Psychologically, *dhikr* frees us from the chains of forgetfulness by arousing, concentrating, and transforming the energies of our unconscious.

Hence, we begin to feel the rhythmic beating of the heart that transforms the energy of the cells within our bodies. Thus, we embrace the remembrance of God, who in turn remembers us. It is through the consciousness of this mutual bond between God and man that embeds the unity in our hearts. *Dhikr* is a means of awakening a slumbering consciousness in order to strengthen our hearts in bringing us nearer to God. The essence of *dhikr* is when the transformation in the heart results in seeking God rather than just seeking from God, in serving God rather than just worshipping God, and in remembering God rather than just reminders about God.

From this transformation, the heart becomes strengthened by the certainty of truth (*haq al-yaqin*), as it has been purified of blemishes and sins. The goal of remembrance is to transform our beings through absorbing the truth. The pure heart (*qalbun saleem*) is now motivated to love all that God loves and to detest all that God detests. *Dhikr* transforms the heart, for it brings ease and strength to attain the serene self (*nafs al-mutma'inna*). When the serene self enters our hearts, the end result is one of peace, harmony, and loving. There are a number of verses in the Qur'an that promote good health and healing of the heart.

> O' mankind! Indeed has come unto you an exhortation from your Lord, and a cure (*for (the diseases)* what is in your breasts and a guidance and mercy for the believers. (Qur'an 10:57)

> And We sent down the Qur'an which is a healing and a mercy unto the believers, but it adds not to the unjust but perdition. (Qur'an 17:82)

In the remembrance (*dhikr*) of God, we purify and find the cure for our diseases.

> Indeed he (*alone*) succeeds who purifies himself. And remembers the name of his Lord and (*regularly*) prays. (Qur'an 87:14–15)

Purifying our hearts from sins, such as arrogance and hatred, occurs when we remember God and ask Him for forgiveness. Humbled, we also pray for God to guide others by also removing sins from their hearts. Through individual self-refinement (*tazkiya*) of our souls, we secure our faith through devotion (*ikhlas*) to God. Our reliance (*tawakkul*) on God guides us to the straight path and manifests itself in seeking God's contentment (*qana'a*), gratitude (*shukr*), generosity (*infaq*), and patience (*sabr*). We seek reliance and remembrance (*dhikr*) by complete obedience to Him. This obedience takes the shape of piety (*taqwah*), love, and loyalty to God.

Essentially, we have a duty to fulfill our obligations (Qur'an 5:1), which results in the purification of the heart. Duty is composed of three levels of obligations: divine obligations (duty to God), mutual obligations (duty to ourselves), and tacit obligations (duty to others). All three obligations are sacred, whether divine, mutual, or tacit. To fulfill these obligations, we must be in total concert with our intention, which is disciplining ourselves toward achieving the mercy of God. In this worldly existence, we cannot isolate these three duties; they are interrelated and must be practiced in consonance with each other (Turfe 1996).

Fulfillment of Obligations

Duty to God: We must strive in the way of God and seek His mercy through piety (*taqwah*). Not only must we be cognizant of God, but we must worship God as well. To obey and serve God is our major duty to Him.

And obey God and His Apostle; and fall into no disputes, lest you lose heart and your power depart; and be patient and persevering: for God is with those who patiently persevere. (Qur'an 8:46)

Duty to Ourselves: We fulfill the duty to ourselves through refinement of our souls (*tazkiya*). Until we know ourselves, we will never reach self-refinement. With self-refinement we attain prosperity (*falah*). Prophet Muhammad said, "Whoever knows himself knows God." Spiritual well-being is the order of the duty we have toward ourselves. While we seek self-refinement of our souls, we must also ensure the best in our mental health and physical health. We have a responsibility to ourselves. We must practice patience (*sabr*) and refrain from the bad things in life—illegal use of drugs, prostitution, and other vices that not only endanger our bodies but our souls as well.

Duty to Others: We also have a duty to our spouses, families, children, relatives, friends, neighbors, coworkers, classmates, the needy, orphans, and many other people with whom we come into contact, whether daily or occasionally.

> By no means shall you attain righteousness unless you give (*freely*) of that which you love; and whatever you give, of a truth God knows it well. (Qur'an 3:92)

The ultimate test of charity is seen here—to give up something we value greatly. What we give up may be our property, possessions, or just a small token or gesture of kindness. The greatest gift we can give is our personal time—to be patient and make time to help the poor, the needy, and orphans, as well as time to teach our children the religion of Islam.

Tazkiya brings about purity through self-refinement of the soul. One who is pious (*taqwah*) is pure, and one who genuinely repents (*tauba*) can achieve purity, provided that person refrains from sinning in the future. *Tazkiya* enables people to repent and to sustain them in their repentance. It also enables people to be firm and steadfast in their piety. *Tazkiya* comes full circle through its *takhliyah* (making the heart empty from everything and purifying it) and *tahliyah* (beautifying the heart and adorning it through prayer and remembrance (*dhikr*) of God. In essence, *tazkiya* is the science of the pure heart (*qalbun saleem*). Hence, paradise is for those who purify themselves.

By remembering (*dhikr*) God, we will have initiated the initial step in the healing process. In *dhikr*, there is a transformation of the consciousness of mind and heart from outward external thoughts to inward self of intention, meditation, awareness, and recitation of the Qur'an, prayer, supplications (*du'a*), and attributes of God.

The virtue of *dhikr* necessitates us to be responsible for our actions. The *dhikr* of God carries immense rewards and blessings. The peace of mind from *dhikr* results in the serenity of the heart and elevates our spirituality. The more we invoke the remembrance of God, the greater our nearness to Him. The more we neglect His remembrance, the greater we distance ourselves from Him. The effects of *dhikr* are immense. *Dhikr* cures our psychological disorders, purifies our hearts from pollution and tarnish, trains us in patience (*sabr*), and deters us from committing acts of disobedience to God. Because of the effects of self-purification, worshipping, and continuous recital of invocation, God hears our prayers, supplications, and *dhikr*. *Dhikr* of God has numerous benefits. We derive the benefits from this remembrance, some of which are the pleasure of God, nearness of God, God's mercy, God's protection from and forgiveness of sins, comfort and strengthening of the heart, intensified self-control, sharpened insight and concentration, and the ability to ward off evil.

One of the ways to practice *dhikr* and *sabr* is to recite the entire Qur'an during the month of Ramadan. During this month, Muslims become healthier due to a balance in the diet, a more balanced character due to self-restraint, and a reward from God for abstention and submission. During this month, we guard against our temptations and frailties of character by offering ourselves in deep meditation as we cement our metaphysical relationship with God. Fasting increases our resolve and self-restraint, resulting in patience and perseverance against evil. Fasting becomes our struggle and resistance against evil, and with prayer we are guided to the straight path of purity.

During the month of Ramadan, we abstain from food, water, and personal pleasures, as well as parting with some of our wealth as charity. The heart is purified from lust, bigotry, and hate, as well as from indulging in lies, dishonesty, and deception. It is a time to reflect upon the purpose of our existence and to cleanse our hearts from the impurities that have stained it. While fasting cleanses our bodies of impurities, it also purifies our hearts and minds from all impure thoughts and desires. It is a time to test our remembrance of God in order to gain His blessings. In His mercy, God sent the month of Ramadan to purify our hearts and to self-actualize in self-denial. Here, we have the golden opportunity to reach the level of *qalbun saleem* (pure heart) and to sustain its purity even after the month of Ramadan.

Islam mandates humankind to keep their hearts filled with faith. When people become wrapped up in the world of pomp, play, and circumstance, they are unable to distinguish between right and wrong. Hence, a healthy and sound heart weakens because of these distractions and becomes sick. As a result, the sick heart becomes vulnerable to four toxic poisons that infect it: (1) unnecessary talking, (2) unrestrained evil glances, (3) excessive food, and (4) evil company.

Poisons of the Heart

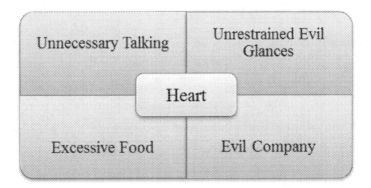

These poisons cause the heart to become sick, thereby contaminating the soul of a believer to fall into ruin. To restore the believer to a sound and healthy heart necessitates getting rid of these toxic poisons. The believer then repents and asks God for His forgiveness. Subsequently, the believer must protect his or her heart by avoiding new toxics.

Preventing unnecessary talking requires the believer to avoid using his or her tongue for ill will and backbiting. Rather, the purification of the tongue guides the believer to speak only in a positive manner.

> When you received it with your tongues and uttered it with your mouths what you had no knowledge of, and you deemed it a light matter; while with God it was grievous. (Qur'an 24:15)

> The Messenger of God said, "Do not talk too much without remembrance of God. Indeed excessive talking without remembrance of God hardens the heart. And indeed the furthest of people from God is the harsh-hearted." (*Jami' At-Tirmidhi*, vol. 4, book 34, chapter 61, Hadith 2411)

God blessed humankind with ears, eyes, and heart so that they can hear, see, and feel the marvels of His creation.

> Say thou (O' Our Apostle Muhammad!) "He it is He who brought you (*into being*) and made for you the ears and the eyes and the hearts; yet how little is it that you thank!" (Qur'an 67:23)

The reason why God gave us two ears but only one tongue was to enable us to listen at least twice as much as we speak. In addition, God gave us two eyes to enable us to see the beauty of nature and a heart from which to feel and understand that beauty. Yet the frailty of humankind fails to thank Him because of complacency, ignorance, or lack of faith. While we have been blessed with these senses, we may still err in being unable to accurately distinguish right from wrong in what we hear and see. In ancient times, humankind was led to believe our world was flat, and they actually believed it was, even in their hearts. Hence, our ears and eyes may deceive us in ascertaining the reality of what we hear and see. When this occurs, we may have a lapse in judgment, and our hearts are put in disarray, utterly confused.

Do we listen more than we talk? Do we have the tendency to turn people off because we just talk on and on, as if in a cadence of exercising our vocal cords so as to drive our audience away? Hence, listening more than talking helps us not only to understand but also to make and sustain our friendships with others. In short, we need to listen to understand before we seek to be understood.

> Imam Ali said, "O' questioner! Listen first, and then understand. Then believe and put what you have learned into practice." (*Al-Kafi*, vol. 2, p. 456)

By hearing with our ears and heart in unison, we can rightly understand the essence of what is being said, as well as the sounds of nature. Yet corruption of the heart enters through the ears and eyes so as to distort the reality and nature of our existence, which is to hear, see, and feel all that God has provided us via His prophets, who taught humankind the meaning of God's scriptures and commands.

Relative to unrestrained evil glances, the Qur'an provides the prescription.

> Say thou (*O' Our Apostle Muhammad!*) unto the believer men that they cast down their gaze and guard their private parts; that is purer for them; verily, God is All-Aware of what (*all*) you do. (Qur'an 24:30)

Do we understand what we see with our eyes? Are we able to see yet fail to live up to God's commands, thereby falling into despair and misery? God gave us eyes to see, in all natural objects, what He envisioned for humankind and to open the spirituality of our eyes to see more clearly the reason for our existence. In effect, God opens a whole set of spiritual senses that helps us see life from His perspective. Just reading a verse from the Qur'an opens many avenues of understanding its meaning. We may have read the same verse many times, and then the truth becomes very clear. The verse was always correct; it was just that our concentration in reading that verse was weak. Once we heightened our concentration and became focused, then we understood the meaning of that verse. In other words, we opened up our spiritual eyes.

To uphold the Islamic personality and all its meaning and manifestations, we must be careful as to how we use our eyes, so as not to corrupt them. For example, we should lower our gazes by restraining them so they don't wander off or dwell upon evil sights or thoughts. In addition, we must not ogle by gazing our eyes on the opposite sex. We must not attend unholy places, such as nightclubs, bars, or sexually deviated places.

> Strain not thine eyes at what We have provided with some of them pairs among them to enjoy, and grieve not for them and lower thy wing (*be gentle*) unto the believers. (Qur'an 15:88)

We should not admire those who are immersed in worldly and materialistic pleasures that are adornments of this world, such as exotic clothing, alcohol consumption, or other acts that are inconsistent with our Islamic personality and behavior. We must forego the pomp and circumstance of an empty life.

> Know you that the life of this world is only a sport and play, a gaiety and a boasting and the lustful-vying in the multiplication of wealth and children, is like unto the rain therewith springs up the vegetation, it pleases the husbandmen; then it is withered away, and thou sees it become yellow, then becomes it stubble crumbling down. And in the Hereafter is a severe chastisement and (*also*) forgiveness from God, and (*His*) pleasures; and naught is the life of this world but means of illusion. (Qur'an 57:20)

People not only spend their lives in this world, but they indulge in showing off, boasting, and piling up riches in rivalry (Qur'an 6:32, 29:64, 47:36). Most of the attractions of the vanities of this world are but trials and tests (Qur'an 3:185). Now that we can see the truth about the reality of this world, with its deceptive distractions and adornments, we should be consistent in our reciting the Qur'an daily so that we receive its reminder (dhikr) about this fleeting and temporary life. Likewise, we should open our ears to the Islamic sermons given by our religious scholars.

A sign of a true Muslim is that he or she avoids excessive food. Eating too much is prohibited in Islam, as it leads to displeasing God and becoming injurious to our health. Of course we should eat, but we need to abstain from stuffing the belly to its fullest, as it would weaken the heart.

> O' children of Adam! Be you adorned at every time of prostration and eat you and drink you and commit you not excesses; verily He (God) loves not the extravagant. (Qur'an 7:31)

Keeping evil company is also prohibited in Islam. Unnecessary companionship is a chronic disease that causes much harm. Choose your friends wisely, and ensure that they are righteous.

> And on the day when the heavens shall burst asunder with cloud and the angels be sent down, descending (*in ranks*), the kingdom that day in truth shall belong to the Beneficent Lord; and the day for the infidels shall be very hard. And on the day when the unjust one shall bite his hands saying: "Oh! Would that I had taken with the Apostle the (*same right*) path!" (Qur'an 25:25–27)

Therefore, if the soul abandons the truthful ones and instead becomes familiar with sinners and being heedless of God, then it is doomed. Hence, we need to invoke our Islamic personality in order to protect the healthy heart by guarding it against negative energy and constantly filling it with positive energy.

Chapter 13

Islamic Personality of
the Pure Heart

The Islamic personality emanates from the pure heart (*qalbun saleem*). Within our personality structure, we have individual selves. Each of these selves has a unique system. For example, the self has its own goals and priorities. Each has its own perceptions and motives. Each has its own style and developmental cycles. Each has its own limits of tolerance and emotional sensitivity. Dynamic and interactive, our subselves can communicate with each other to form a decision. When making decisions, the subselves condition our true basic selves.

We are not born with a personality. Our personality is formed, shaped, and developed in the framework of our relationships with our family and environment. Personality is consistent of individuality, as we behave in a manner consistent within each of us. It is this consistency of our behavior that defines the kind of personality with which we are associated. Our personalities are a product of our genetics and environment. For example, our personalities may be one of tolerance or aggression. Nonetheless, while personality traits may be acquired from parents at birth, our environment is a major influence on how these traits unfold. A child may be born into a Muslim family, but his environment may influence whether he develops into a good Muslim. Character traits form the personality pattern, which is a product of heredity and learning available in our environments. Therefore, while genetic makeup may serve as the foundation of our personalities, relationships within the environment shape our personalities.

People often see themselves differently from how others perceive them. How we see ourselves is referred to as the self-concept, which can be either positive or negative. A positive self-concept results in feeling good, while a negative self-concept results in feeling bad. The self-concept consists of our thoughts, attitudes, and feelings about ourselves (i.e., our perceived self-worth). Like the personality, the self-worth is also a product of our heredity and environment. Factors such as education, religion, family background, and overall health have a bearing on our self-concepts.

The basic self-concept is the person's concept of what he or she is. The person arrives at this after considering such things as physical appearance, strengths or weaknesses, position in a community, values, and aspirations. The self-concept is an important step toward purifying the heart and the Islamic personality (Turfe 2004). Let's examine some of the strengths and weaknesses of the self-concept in regard to the Islamic personality and their impact on the pure heart (*qalbun saleem*).

Impact of Self-Concept on the Pure Heart (*Qalbun Saleem*)

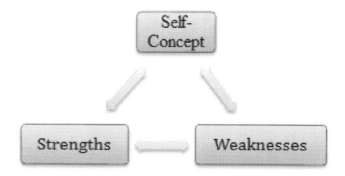

Strengths

Devout	Ethical	Honorable
Righteous	Courageous	Passionate
Truthful	Trustworthy	Chaste
Knowledgeable	Empathetic	Gentle
Patient	Charitable	Hopeful
Prudent	Respectful	Humble
Just	Peaceful	Enlightened

Weaknesses

Insincere	Immoral	Shameful
Sinful	Cowardly	Indifferent
Dishonest	Corrupt	Impure
Ignorant	Hard-hearted	Harsh
Impatient	Inconsiderate	Pessimistic
Reckless	Insolent	Arrogant
Unjust	Violent	Intolerant

The ideal self-concept, however, consists of ideas of what we would like to be or what we believe we ought to be. It may be realistic if it is within reach or unrealistic if it is out of reach. For example, someone may want to be a physician but has not prepared academically for that career. Someone may want to be a professional football player but does not have the size, strength, speed, and agility to become one.

Family influences the development of the personality, both directly and indirectly. One direct influence is the deliberate effort parents make in molding the child's behaviors to conform to societal expectations. The parents use reinforcements such as rewards and punishments to make their teachings effective. One indirect influence is role modeling. Here, the child identifies with and emulates the behavior of an older family member. As a result, the child is likely to develop desirable or undesirable personality traits as he tries to mimic the behaviors of the admired family member.

Development of the Islamic Personality

We are given sound and pure hearts (*qalbun saleem*) upon birth. When we commit sins and disobey God, we are injuring the heart, slowly destroying it. However, if we truly repent, our hearts will start to recover toward becoming healthy and pure again (Qur'an 10:57). The heart that is healthy is able to recognize the truth and lead the rest of the organs and limbs toward practicing the actions of truth and faith. *Qalbun saleem* knows that God is the truth, as it seeks His guidance and mercy so as to not injure itself or deviate from the straight path (Qur'an 3:8). Toward this end, we need to develop unity within ourselves by holding fast to the *Rope of God*. One of the ways in which we can achieve this is by developing an Islamic personality.

> Therefore, be patient with what they say and celebrate (*constantly*) the praises of the Lord, before the rising of the sun, and before it's setting; yea, celebrate them for part of the hours of the night and at the sides of the day: that thou may have (*spiritual*) joy. (Qur'an 20:130)

Evil hovers around us. We must be patient and ask God for guidance so that we can avoid evil and remove its stains from the pure heart. The Islamic personality makes the believer cherish human dignity and prestige and accept his or her responsibilities as a Muslim. The best example of the Islamic personality is that of Prophet Mohammad and his progeny.

The justification of religious morality—that is, Islamic morality—promises the continuance of life in the hereafter for the morally good individuals. In Islam, there is no distinction between theoretical morality and physical morality. Morality deals with determining right from wrong. Morality is composed of virtues. Faith, righteous deeds, truth, and patience are the basic virtues of Islamic morality and the pure heart (*qalbun saleem*). Individuals gain eternal happiness through moral virtues. Prophet Mohammad said, "My religion is based on cleanliness."

Cleanliness here does not refer only to our daily washing and cleansing of our bodies. There is a higher meaning to this message, a meaning that attaches itself to the inner purity of the soul. We must cleanse our thoughts and our hearts in order to attain ultimate and final perfection. In striving toward perfection through self-purification, God will guide us.

> And those who strive in Our (*Cause*) - We will certainly guide them to Our Paths: for verily God is with those who do right. (Qur'an 29:69)

And the path is the straight path (*sirat al-mustaqim*). We must free ourselves from the spider's web of this frail world. We must walk the path of struggle against immoral tendencies that damage the pure heart. All that we can do is strive in the way of God. With firmness of purpose, determination, and patience, we can attain the mercy of God.

In addition to cleanliness, other traits help nurture our Islamic personalities. For example, while the ideal Islamic personality is one of moral excellence, it is also the preservation of self-respect and dignity by way of piety. It is one of righteousness and faith. It is one of adhering to the beliefs and practices in Islam. For example, we study the rules of *hajj* before making the pilgrimage. When we return from the *hajj*, our awareness is heightened, our hearts are purified, and our lifestyles exemplify that of a Muslim.

The ideal Islamic personality is one who believes his or her sole purpose in life is to worship God and to seek the pleasure and guidance of God. The ideal Islamic personality is one where faith leads to good deeds, and good deeds lead to faith. By helping others, he is, in effect, helping himself become a better Muslim. He sincerely concentrates on every aspect of his life, as he continues to understand the beauty and wisdom of Islam. He reads the Qur'an so that he can enlighten his pure heart (*qalbun saleem*), and he is grateful for the bounties and blessings God has bestowed upon him. Therefore, he continues to remember God and to win the satisfaction of the Creator.

Other examples of the ideal Islamic personality are when the Muslim is truthful, does not cheat, is not envious, is sincere, and keeps his promises. He is gentle toward people, compassionate, and merciful. He is tolerant, forgiving, and patient. He refrains from backbiting and slander and avoids suspicion. He is humble and modest and strives for reconciliation between Muslims (Turfe 2004).

Revolving Hierarchy of the Islamic Personality

As a guideline, I have formulated the Revolving Hierarchy of the Islamic Personality, which begins with faith (*iman*) and ends with endurance (*sabr*), and then proceeds back to faith (*iman*) by way of the pure heart (*qalbun saleem*). This is based on the four virtues in chapter 103 of the Qur'an, which inculcates within individuals the four primary virtues of faith, righteous deeds, truth, and patience or endurance. Imam Ali said,

> Practice endurance and patience; it is to faith what the head is to the body. There is no good in a body without a head, or in faith without endurance. (*Nahjul Balagha*)

Tantamount to this circular effect is the analogy of proceeding from theory to fact and then back to theory again. The Pure Heart (*Qalbun Saleem*) Revolving Hierarchy of Islamic Personality is composed of six stages (Turfe 1996):

1. *asas an-nafs* (self-foundation)
2. *aman an-nafs* (self-security)
3. *waee an-nafs* (self-awareness)
4. *tahkeek an-nafs* (self-achievement)
5. *retha an-nafs* (self-satisfaction)
6. *idrak an-nafs* (self-realization)

Pure Heart (*Qalbun Saleem*) Revolving
Hierarchy of Islamic Personality

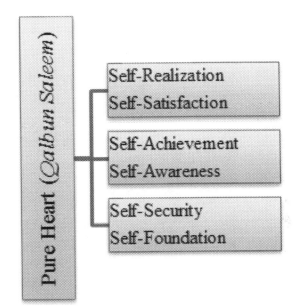

There are at least two theories as to how we absorb these criteria. One theory given by a number of religious scholars is that God makes these and other criteria prior to our existence. In our lives we practice the criteria that God gave us at birth. Another theory postulated by several philosophers is that we are not given these criteria at birth but we develop these criteria as we progress in our lives. What this means is that we choose during our lives whether to develop some or all of these criteria. What is important in either theory is that we can practice these criteria according to the values given us by God. As we search for meaning in our lives, it is these values that make for a better Islamic personality.

These criteria of the Islamic personality are intertwined with each other. Self-foundation is the basic need, while self-security and self-awareness are deficit needs. Self-achievement, self-satisfaction, and self-realization are growth needs. As these needs are dependent on each other, they cannot be separated. They comprise the total Islamic personality. For example, assume that we have progressed to the growth need of self-satisfaction, and suddenly the deficit need of self-security is threatened. Therefore, we have to regress back in the hierarchy and fulfill the deficit need of self-security. Growth needs must be pursued once the requirements of the lower needs are fulfilled.

With faith (*iman*) as the self-foundation, we proceed upward until we attain self-realization by way of endurance (*sabr*), and then we proceed back to faith (*iman*). We proceed upward and downward on the continuum of the revolving hierarchy by way of the pure heart (*qalbun saleem*). We always need to reinforce and strengthen our pure hearts (*qalbun saleem*) and, therefore, our Islamic personalities by absorbing ourselves in these criteria (Turfe 2004).

Having faith leads us to practice and being secure in at least the five requirements of prayer, fasting, alms, pilgrimage, and struggle. With this, we become aware of truth as we seek knowledge, understanding, and wisdom. The straight path via worship and piety results in the self-achievement of righteous deeds, respect, and prosperity. Prosperity or salvation occurs when we have freed ourselves from selfishness and basic desires, thereby purifying our hearts. Prosperity emanates from our self-achievement. If we are purified through worship and are humble and patient, we will attain prosperity and success.

> But those will prosper who purify themselves, and glorify the name of their Guardian Lord, and (*lift their hearts*) in prayer. (Qur'an 87:14–15)

> O' you who believe! Persevere in patience and constancy; vie in such perseverance; strengthen each other; and fear God that you may prosper. (Qur'an 3:200)

Tranquility and happiness are the levels of self-satisfaction that arise from self-achievement. At the zenith of the fulfillment of these needs is self-realization through endurance. Similarly, moving from endurance downward through each of the six categories makes us more cognizant of our roles as Muslims and of our contribution toward Islam.

Self-realization of the basic needs of the pure heart (*qalbun saleem*) will ensure that it remains sound and healthy. These basic needs are (1) know oneself, (2) make intention for the sake of God, and (3) adopt good habits.

Self-Realization of the Pure Heart (*Qalbun Saleem*)

Know Oneself

↓

Make Intention for Sake of God

↓

Adopt Good Habits

Self-awareness will enable us to know who we are and the purpose of our existence. Our intention to change for the better should emanate from the remembrance of God and to serve Him unconditionally. Hence, preventing bad habits by adopting good habits, such as repenting (*qalbun muneeb*) for past sins, praying, fasting, charity, pilgrimage, performing righteous deeds, reading the Qur'an, and reciting supplications (*du'a*) is a great start. Constant adherence and performance of these good habits will lead toward the self-realization of cleansing and purifying the heart (*qalbun saleem*) and perfecting (*ihsan*) the soul.

Moral judgment is applied to all activities, which results in a single, undivided Islamic personality. Through prayer, we can strengthen our Islamic personalities and resolve in order to grapple with evil and overcome its dastardly venom that plagues the pure heart (*qalbun saleem*). Struggle (*jihad*) manifests itself in prayer.

> Enjoin prayer on thy people, and be constant therein.
> We ask thee not to provide sustenance: We provide it
> for thee. But (*fruit of*) the Hereafter is for righteousness.
> (Qur'an 20:132)

True, God provides sustenance for all, just and unjust, in this ephemeral world. But this is a transient existence that ends almost as soon as it begins. So we must be prudent and wise in how we utilize that sustenance and must exercise our patience and struggle in the way of God by doing good and prohibiting evil.

> So persevere in patience for the promise of God is true: and whether We show thee (*in this life*) some part of what We promise them, - or We take thy soul (*to Our mercy*) (*before that*), - (*in any case*) it is to Us that they shall (all) return. (Qur'an 40:77)

In order for the pure heart (*qalbun saleem*) to self-actualize, Muslims have to protect their external behaviors and deeds, their words and thoughts, their feelings and intentions. Truth and virtue are their goals. Justice will prevail. Every soul must return to God for His justice and judgment. Life in this world is very short, but life in the hereafter is eternal. God provides sustenance to the righteous in the hereafter. The unjust are doomed to a dark and ghastly world of punishment. The Muslim's relationship with God must be a pure heart that is immersed in love and obedience.

Immersion of the Pure Heart (Qalbun Saleem)

Immersion is a Muslim's state of being deeply engaged and absorbed by his or her emotional reaction to the spiritual world in terms of feeling as if he or she is actually a part of the spiritual world. With its vibrating energy, immersion expands the mind, opens the heart, and activates the power of the soul. Through prayer, meditation, and fasting, immersion is a gateway to inner wisdom and awakening the pure heart (*qalbun saleem*). Immersion will empower, uplift, and transform the awakened pure heart so as to turn our weaknesses and threats into strengths and opportunities to meet the daily challenges of life. Through immersion, the pure heart (*qalbun saleem*) is nourished, and the Islamic personality is inspired and fulfilled. Even the immersion of sound, as we listen to recitations from the Qur'an, awakens our pure hearts. The immersion of vibratory sounds heightens our inner awareness and culminates into healing and relaxation of the pure heart.

Ablution (*wudu'*) is the ritual washing performed by Muslims before prayer. One of the pillars of Islam is that Muslims pray five times a day. Before commencing with each prayer, Muslims are expected to first perform the purification ritual of ablution, requiring that they wash their faces, hands, arms, and feet. Ablution by immersion means that we should dip our faces and hands into water, with the intention of performing *wudu'*. Relative to performing the ablution in preparation for prayer, there are two methods, either the sequence bath (*ghusl tartibi*) by washing requisite parts of the body or immersion bath (*ghusl irtimasi*) by washing the entire body with water at the same time. With each method, water cleanses the body.

The lifeblood of our existence is water because without water there is no life. Water is energy, and energy is life. Ablution removes the impurities by purifying the body, mind, soul, and heart with water. Even when we seek relaxation, we instinctively connect with the energy of water; for example, swimming, listening to the sounds of the ocean's rolling waves, being enrapt by the serenity of a waterfall, or just taking a bath. In effect, the immersion of water is healing and therapeutic, as well as purification of the heart and refinement of the Islamic personality.

Before performing the ablution, Muslims must first make their intention (*niyyah*) to pray. That intention is evoked from the heart, as Muslims become immersed in the divine and detached from all worldly attachments. Muslims must harness the power of their intention. Our remembrance (*dhikr*) of God has no value if the intention is impure. Before we begin our remembrance of God, we make our intention to do so. In the consciousness of one who is immersed in the divine love of God, there is no deception, no narrowness of caste or creed, and no boundaries of any kind. Our perfection is attained through immersion in the ocean of God's forgiveness.

When people are completely immersed in the world of materialism and not accountable for their actions, they affect a spiritual death within their hearts. So immersed in amusement, they have become unaware of reality. At the same time, they are more involved with everything around them because they are fully immersed in the current of life. Usually, they are immersed in the problems of the past or the worries of the future, and they base their entire existence on them. They often find themselves constrained to negative thoughts and troubled emotions.

However, they can immerse themselves in talking about their problems, or they can ascertain what those problems contain. As a result, they would then embrace the inner struggle and be directed to the straight path of happiness. Hence, they become more attuned to explore, to learn, and to immerse themselves in the resurgence, thereby enhancing the self-esteem of the Islamic personality and purifying their hearts. Moreover, they will become deeply entrenched within the inner depths of their pure hearts. Prophet Muhammad said,

> "In the body there is a piece of flesh. If it is healthy, the entire body will be healthy. But if it is corrupt, the entire body will be corrupt. Verily it is the heart." (*Sahih Muslim*, vol. 4, book 22, chapter 20, Hadith 4094)

Once they understand the root of their difficulties, then ease will transform and free them from the darkness of their despair. They will, in effect, begin to understand and see the manifestation of their pure hearts and purpose in life. In essence, they will become immersed in the present and break away from the shackles of stress and worry. Therefore, they will understand and accept reality as it is, rather than wish it away. Furthermore, they will not seek to change the world but to change themselves, which is within their power to do so, resulting in the contentment of the heart. Immersion engages them to experiences that provide clear understanding of their existence and self-actualization of the Islamic personality.

Epilogue

Life is complicated. How do I get a pure heart (*qalbun saleem*) and keep it? Why is it important to have a pure and clean heart? These questions were discussed in the context of experiencing God's presence, becoming holy, remaining focused in life, and guarding and protecting our relationship with God.

Being pure in heart involves having a unified heart toward God. A pure heart has no insincerity, no deceit, and no hidden motives. The pure heart is a transparent heart, evident by a steadfast desire to please God in everything. The pure heart is both an external purity of behavior and internal purity of soul. In essence, the heart is our center of being.

Have we ever had our hearts cleansed? To cleanse our hearts is to be sensitive to constantly remembering (*dhikr*) God in our prayers and supplications so that He, in turn, protects and strengthens the purity of our hearts. The heart is like a computer. A virus may be disregarded or ignored as it infects and eats into the data and other functions of the computer. Similarly, a sin is like a virus in that it will infect and eat into the fort of the heart, causing it to further transgress, thereby staining and losing the pure heart (*qalbun saleem*).

The success in the hereafter depends upon the purification of our hearts in this life. Our Islamic personality emanates from the pure heart (*qalbun saleem*). We must purify our hearts from spiritual sins, such as egoism, envy, hatred, pessimism, greed, arrogance, and doubt. In their place, we must embellish and beautify the heart with spiritual virtues, such as patience, empathy, humility, generosity, compassion, contentment, and self-denial.

Qalbun saleem is not simply the organ of emotions, feelings, and desires; it is one that comprehends knowledge, wisdom, and the soul. In effect, it is the seat of the intellect that is heart-knowledge rather than mind-knowledge. The conscious heart is patient, concentrated, and disciplined; it abstains from sins and commits its will to the will of God.

Intention is the spark within the heart. If the intention is corrupt, then the heart is corrupt, thereby nullifying any good deed. However, if the heart is healthy and sound, then good deeds are sincere and honest. If the heart is dead, acceptance and implementation of the teachings of the Qur'an can restore its life. The Qur'an is a reminder (*dhikr*) for humankind to remember God and is nourishment of our souls to sustain the pure heart (*qalbun saleem*). Therefore, we should firmly hold to the Rope of God (Qur'an), which is a direct path toward Him. There will come a day when nothing will benefit us, except a pure heart.

> The Day when will avail not wealth or sons, save him who comes unto God with a heart submissive. (Qur'an 26:88–89)

Appendix A

SELECTED OCCURRENCES OF THE HEART IN THE QUR'AN

2:7	3:159	8:2	9:125	18:14	26:88	33:51	47:21	59:10
2:10	3:167	8:10	9:127	18:28	26:89	33:53	47:24	59:14
2:74	4:63	8:11	10:57	18:33	26:193	33:60	47:29	61:5
2:88	4:155	8:12	10:74	18:57	26:194	34:23	48:4	63:3
2:93	5:7	8:24	10:88	21:3	26:200	35:38	48:11	64:11
2:97	5:13	8:43	11:5	22:32	27:74	37:83	48:12	66:4
2:118	5:41	8:49	11:23	22:34	28:10	37:84	48:18	67:13
2:204	5:52	8:63	13:27	22:35	28:69	39:7	48:26	67:23
2:225	5:113	8:70	13:28	22:46	29:10	39:22	49:3	74:31
2:260	6:25	9:8	14:37	22:52	29:49	39:23	49:7	79:6
2:283	6:43	9:15	14:42	22:53	30:59	39:45	49:14	79:7
3:7	6:46	9:45	14:43	22:54	31:23	40:18	50:32	79:8
3:8	6:110	9:60	15:12	23:60	32:9	40:35	50:33	79:9

3:103	6:112	9:64	15:47	23:63	33:4	41:5	50:37	83:14
3:119	6:113	9:77	16:22	23:78	33:5	42:24	53:11	104:6
3:126	7:43	9:87	16:78	24:36	33:10	45:23	57:16	104:7
3:151	7:100	9:93	16:106	24:37	33:12	46:26	57:27	114:5
3:154	7:101	9:110	17:36	24:50	33:26	47:16	58:22	
3:156	7:179	9:117	17:46	25:32	33:32	47:20	59:2	

Source: Qur'an

Appendix B

Selected Verses in the Qur'an on the Heart

God has sealed up their hearts and their hearing; and upon their sight is a covering, and for them is a great chastisement (2:7).

In their heart is a disease, and God increases their disease, for them is a painful chastisement, because of the lie they were saying (2:10).

Thenceforth were your hearts hardened as stones or harder still; for verily of stones are some from which gush forth streams; others there are which split asunder and from them comes out water; and of them there are some that fall down for fear of God; and God is not heedless of what you do (2:74).

And they say: "Our hearts are covered." Nay! God has cursed them for their disbelief; so little is that they believe (2:88).

Say (*O' Our Apostle Muhammad*) whoso is an enemy to Gabriel; for, verily it is he who has brought it unto thy heart by God's (*command*) confirming what had (*already*) been (revealed) before and guidance and glad tidings to the believers (2:97).

And if you be on a journey and you find not a scribe, then take a pledge with possession; but if one of you trusts the other, let the one trusted fulfill his trust, and take shelter in God his Lord; and conceal not evidence; and whosoever conceals it, then surely his heart is sinful; and verily God knows all that you do (2:283).

(*They pray*) "Our Lord! Suffer not our hearts to perverse after Thou has guided (*aright*) and grant us from unto Thee mercy, for verily Thou, and Thou (*Alone*) art the Ever-Bestower" (3:8).

And hold you fast by the Rope of God all together, and be not divided (*among yourselves*) and remember the bounty of God bestowed upon you, when you were enemies (*of each other*). He united your hearts together with (*mutual*) love, and thus by His favor you have become brethren and (*while*) you were on the brink of the pit of the Hell-Fire then He delivered you therefrom; thus does God clearly explain His signs for you, so that you may be guided (3:103).

Verily God well knows whatever is in (*people's*) breasts (3:119).

We will cast a dread into the hearts of the disbelievers because they have associated with God, that for which He has sent down no authority and their abode shall be the fire; and how bad is the abode of the unjust (3:151).

Thus it is a mercy of God that thou art lenient unto them: had thou been severe and hard-hearted, they would surely have dispersed away from around thee; therefore, forgive them and seek pardon for them; and take their counsel in the affair; but when thou art resolved, then put thou thy trust in God; for God loves those who trust (*in Him*) (3:159).

So for their breaking their covenant and their denial of the signs of God, and their slaying the apostles unjustly and their saying, "Our hearts are covered;" Nay! God has set a seal upon them for their disbelief, so they believe not but a little (4:155).

(O' Our Apostle Muhammad!) Let not those who hasten in infidelity grieve thee, of those who say, "We believe" with their mouths and their hearts believe not ... (5:41).

So see thou those in whose hearts is disease hastening towards them, saying "We fear lest a reverse (of fortune) befall us;" but belike God brings about a victory (*for thee*) or (*some*) thing from Himself, then will they be regretting for what they hid in their selves (5:52).

And of them are those who hearken unto thee, and We have cast veils over their hearts lest they understand it, and a heaviness into their ears; and (*even*) if they see every sign they will not believe in it; to the extent that when they come to thee they only dispute with thee, those who disbelieve say: "This is naught but the legends of the ancients" (6:25).

Say: "Think you, that if God takes away your hearing and your sight and seals on your hearts, who is the god other than God that can bring it (*again*) to you?" See thou, how We display (explaining) the signs yet they turn aside (6:46).

And We will turn (*aside*) their hearts and their visions, even as they did not believe in it the first time, and We will leave them in their contumacy, wandering blindly on (6:110).

Is it not (*a lesson*) guiding (*enough*) for those who inherit the earth after its former people that if We please We would afflict (*too*) for their sins, and set a seal on their hearts that they would not hearken? (7:100).

These towns – We relate unto thee (*some*) of their events, and (*that*) indeed did come unto them their apostles with clear evidences (*miracles*), but they would believe not in what they belied from before; thus does set God a seal on the hearts of the infidels (7:101).

Indeed We have created for hell many of the jinn and the men. They have hearts (*but*) they understand not with it; and they have eyes (*but*) they see not with it; and they have ears (*but*) they hear not with it; and they are like cattle, nay, more astray. These are they the heedless ones (7:179).

Verily believers are only those who when God is mentioned their hearts get thrilled, and when unto them are recited His signs they increase them in faith, and on God (*alone*) do they rely (8:2).

[A]nd know you that God gets (*always there*) in between man and his heart … (8:24).

Caused He affection between their hearts; had thou spent all that is in the earth thou could not have caused that affection between their hearts, but God caused affection between them … (8:63).

"If God knows any good in your hearts, He will give you better than what has been taken away from you, and (*He*) will forgive you …" (8:70).

And remove He the rage of the hearts; and God turns (*merciful*) unto whomsoever He pleases … (9:15).

Only they ask leave of thee (*to be exempt*) who believe not in God and the Last Day (*of judgment*), and their hearts are in doubt, hence in their doubt they are tossed to and fro (9:45).

The hypocrites fear lest a 'Sura' should be sent about them declaring openly unto them what is (*there really*) in their hearts. Say! "Scoff you! Verily God brings forth what you fear" (9:64).

Prefer they to be with those (*women, children, and the sick*) who stay behind for a seal has been set on their hearts therefore they understand not (9:87).

O' mankind! Indeed have come unto you an exhortation from your Lord, and a cure for (*the diseases*) what is in your breasts and a guidance and mercy for the believers (10:57).

Thus do We seal up the hearts of the transgressors (10:74).

And those who believe and their hearts are set at rest by God's remembrance; certainly by God's remembrance (*only*) are the hearts set at rest (13:28).

"And We will root out whatever rancor be in their hearts, (*they shall be*) as brothers, on dignified couches, face to face" (15:47).

Your God is One God; and those who believe not in the hereafter, their hearts are repulsive (*against the truth*), and they are men of pride (16:22).

He who disbelieves in God after his belief in Him, save he who is compelled while his heart remains steadfast with the faith, but he who opens his breast for infidelity, on these is the wrath of God; for them shall be a great torment (16:106).

And pursue thou not that which thou has not the knowledge of; verily, the hearing and the sight and the heart, all these shall be questioned about it (17:36).

When thou (*O' Our Apostle Muhammad!*) recites the Qur'an, We set between thee and those who believe not in the hereafter a hidden veil; and we have set on their hearts coverings lest they should understand it (*the Qur'an*) and in their ears a heaviness, and when thou mentions thy Lord alone, in (*reciting*) the Qur'an, turn they their backs in aversion (17:45–46).

And restrain thou thyself with those who call unto their Lord morning and evening seeking His pleasure, and let not thy eyes turn away from them, aspiring the pomp of the life of this world; and obey not him whose heart We have made unmindful of Our remembrance, and he who follows his inclination, and his case has transgressed the limits (18:28).

That (*shall be so*), and whoever respects the signs of God verily it is (*the reflection*) of the piety of the hearts (22:32).

And give glad tidings unto the humble ones, who when God is mentioned, get thrilled their hearts (*with awe for His Glory*) ... (22:34–35).

What! Have not they travelled in the earth that they should have hearts to understand them with, or ears to hear them with? For verily blind are not the eyes but blind are the hearts that are in the breasts (22:46).

And We sent not before thee (*O' Our Apostle Muhammad!*) any apostle or prophet, but when he recited (*the message*) the Satan did cast his recitation (*to create error*); but God cancels that, which the Satan casts, then God does establish His signs; and verily God is All-Knowing, All-Wise. So that he may make that which casts the Satan a trial unto those in whose hearts is disease and those whose hearts are hard; and verily, the unjust are in a schism far (*away from the truth*). And that may know those who have been given the knowledge that it (*Qur'an*) is the truth from thy Lord, so they may believe in it and may humble unto it their hearts; and verily, God guides those who believe, unto the right path (22:52–54).

And those who give what they give (*in charity*) while their hearts thrilled for fear that unto their Lord they must return (23:60).

The day when will avail not wealth or son, save him who comes unto God with a heart submissive (26:88–89).

And the heart of the mother of Moses became tranquil; she was about to disclose it had We not strengthened her heart so that she might be of the believers (*in Our promise*) (28:10).

And indeed have We set forth for the people, in this Qur'an, every kind of similitude; and if thou bring unto them a sign, certainly will say those who disbelieve: "You are naught but a false claimant." Thus does God set a seal on the hearts of those who know not? (30:58–59).

God has made not for any man two hearts in his breast ... (33:4).

When came they upon you from above you and from below you, and were turned dull the eyes, and reached to the throats the hearts, and you did imagine about God diverse thoughts (33:10).

And verily of his persuasion was Abraham. When came he unto his Lord with a submissive heart? (37:83–84).

God has sent down the best recital, a Book consistent (*in its parts*) with iteration, at which do shudder the skins of those who fear their Lord, then get softened their skins and their hearts unto the remembrance of God ... (39:23).

Those who dispute about the Signs of God without any authority having come unto them; are greatly hated by God and by those who believe; thus God sets a seal over every heart which is arrogant and haughty (40:35).

These are they on whose hearts has God set a seal, and follow they their vain desires (47:16).

What! Reflect they not on the Qur'an? Nay! On (their) hearts are (set) their locks (47:24).

He it is who sent down tranquility into the hearts of the faithful that they might add further faith to their faith ... (48:4).

Verily those who lower their voices in the presence of the Apostle of God, they are those whose hearts God has proved for their guarding (*themselves against evil*) ... (49:3).

But God has endeared the faith unto you, and made it attractive in your hearts and made abhorrent unto you disbelief and transgression ... (49:7).

Say the deep desert Arabs, "We believe." Say thou (*unto them*): "You believed not, but say you, "We have submit, for faith has not yet entered your hearts ..." (49:14).

And the Garden (*Paradise*) shall be brought near unto the pious ones, not far (*from thence*). "This is what you have been promised; (*this is*) for every one who turns (*frequently*) unto God, (*and*) guards (*His limits*)"; "Who fears the Beneficent God in secret, and comes (*unto Him*) with a heart, turned (*to Him in devotion*)." "Enter it you in peace, this is the Day of eternal life!" (50:31–34).

Verily in this is a reminder for him who has a heart or he gives ear with the presence of his mind (50:37).

Has not the time come, for those who believe that their hearts become humble for the remembrance of God and what has come down of the truth? And (*that*) they should not be like unto those who were given the Book before, but (*when*) lengthened the ages passed over them, so it hardened their hearts; and many of them are transgressors (57:16).

Then We made Our apostles to follow in their footsteps, and sent We after them Jesus, son of Mary, and We gave him the Evangel; and We put into the hearts of those who followed him kindness and compassion; but (*as to*) the monastic life, they invented it themselves ... (57:27).

For God has inscribed faith in their hearts and has strengthened them with a Spirit from Himself ... (58:22).

They will fight not against you in a body except in towns fortified or from behind walls. Their fighting among themselves is severe; thou may deem them united, but their hearts are divided. That is because they are a people who understand not (59:14).

[B]ut when (*yet*) went they astray, God (*too*) allowed their hearts (*to astray*); and God guides not the people who transgress (61.5).

[A]nd who believes in Allah, He guides his heart ... (64:11).

Nay! Rather, has rusted their hearts, what they used to do (83:14).

Say, "I seek refuge in the Lord of the people! The King of the people! From the evil of the Satan (*slinking whisperer*), who whispers into the breasts (*hearts*) of the people, (be he) from among the Jinn and the men? (114:1–6).

Source: S. V. Mir Ahmed Ali. *The Holy Qur'an: Text, Translation and Commentary.* Elmhurst, New York: Tahrike Tarsile Qur'an Inc., 1995.

Appendix C

SELECTED SHI'A HADITHS ON THE HEART

Al-Kafi and *Bihar al-Anwar*

Al-Kafi, vol. 2, p. 273

Imam al-Baqir said, "Initially there is a white spot and light within the heart of a human being, and as a result of his committing sin, a black spot appears. If the person repents, the black spot gets wiped out, but if he persisted in sinning, the blackness gradually increases ultimately covering the entire white spot; when this happens, the owner of such a heart will never return towards goodness and become manifestation of the verse of the Holy Qur'an: 'Nay, but that which they have earned is rust upon their hearts.'"

Al-Kafi, vol. 2, p. 422, "kitab al-Iman wa al-kufr" "bab fi Zulmah qalb al-munafiq," Hadith 1

Imam al-Sadiq said, "You see some people who are so perfect in eloquence that they don't err in [the use of a single letter like] *lam* or *waw*, while their hearts are darker than a gloomy night, and there are some people who cannot express what is in their hearts, yet their heart is radiant like a lamp."

Al-Kafi, vol. 2, p. 422, "kitab al-Iman wa al-kufr" "bab fi Zulmah qalb al-munafiq," Hadith 2

As to the heart wherein is faith and hypocrisy, they were a people who lived in Ta'if; so if one of them should die in the state of hypocrisy, he would perish, and should he die in the state of faith, he would attain salvation.

Al-Kafi, vol. 2, p. 614, "kitab fadl al-Qur'an," "bab tartil al-Qur'an bi al-sawt al-hasan," Hadith 1

Muhammad ibn Ya'qab (al-Kulayni) reported with his *isnad* from 'Abd Allah ibn Sulayman that he said: "I asked Abu 'Abd Allah, may peace be upon him, concerning the statement of God, the Exalted, 'And recite the Qur'an with tartil.' He replied, 'The Commander of the Faithful, may peace be upon him said, '(it means:) Recite it in a clear and distinct manner: neither with impetus like poetry is recited, nor in a slow-moving manner so that the words are scattered like sand. Read in such a manner as to arouse and startle your callous hearts, and your aim should not be to get to the end of the *surah*.'"

Al-Kafi, Hadith No. 5

Sufyan ibn 'Uyaynah said, "I asked Imam al-Sadiq about the utterance of God, the Exalted and the Glorious, in regard to the Day of Resurrection. 'The day when neither wealth nor sons shall profit except he who comes with a pure heart (Qur'an 26:88–89).' The Imam replied, 'A pure heart is one that meets its Lord in a state in which there is none in it except Him.' Then he added: 'every heart in which there is shirk or doubt shall fail. Indeed, He has meant by it (the purity of heart) nothing except zuhd in regard to the world so that their hearts may be made ready for the Hereafter.'"

Bihar al-Anwar, vol. 70, p. 51

Imam Mohammad al-Baqir said, "There are three kinds of hearts: First Type: Reversed heart that lacks feelings for any sort of righteous deeds. Such heart is the heart of an unbeliever. Second Type: The heart that contains a black spot in which a war is being waged between the truth and falsehood, and whichever becomes victorious will take over the heart's control. Third Type: The conquered heart in which there is a lighted lamp that is never going to be turned off. Such a heart is the heart of a believer."

Bihar al-Anwar, vol. 70, p. 51

Imam Ja'far al-Sadiq quoted from the holy prophet: "The darkness of the heart is the worst kind of darkness."

Bihar al-Anwar, vol. 70, p. 51

Imam Ali, in his last will, addressed his son: "Oh my son! The poverty is one of the most horrible calamities. But still severe than poverty is the bodily sickness; and the sickness of soul is harsher than the bodily sickness. Plenty of wealth is one of God's blessings, but sound health is better than that, and the piety of the heart is even superior than sound health."

Bihar al-Anwar, vol. 70, p. 53

Imam Ali Zein al-Abideen (al-Sajjad) said, "A man possesses four eyes, with two apparent eyes he sees the affairs relevant to his world, and with two esoteric eyes sees the affairs related to the next world. Therefore, whenever God desired the good for a believer, He opens his heart's eyes to enable him to witness the hidden world and its mysteries. But when He doesn't desire his welfare, leaves the heart with his esoteric eyes closed."

Bihar al-Anwar, vol. 70, p. 53

Imam Ja'far as-Sadiq said, "The heart possesses two ears, the spirit of belief slowly invites him towards righteous deeds, while the Satan slowly invites him towards evil deeds. Therefore, whoever becomes victorious in this struggle takes over heart's control."

Bihar al-Anwar, vol. 70, p. 54

Imam Mohammad al-Baqir said, "There is nothing worst than sinning for the heart. When the heart is encountered with sin, it struggles against the sin until sin becomes victorious thus making the heart as a reversed heart."

Bihar al-Anwar, vol. 70, p. 59
A narration from Anas bin Malik quotes the holy prophet, who said, "The Prophet David asked God; 'Oh God! All the emperors possess treasure then where is Your treasure?' God-Almighty replied: 'I possess a treasure which is greater than the sky; vaster than the Heaven's firmaments; smells better than the perfumes of Paradise; and is more beautiful than the Celestial Kingdom. Its earth is enlightenment; its sky is belief; its sun is enthusiasm; its moon is love. Its stars are inspiration and attention towards Me; its clouds are reason; its rain is blessing; its fruits are obedience; and its yield is wisdom. My Treasure has four doors, the first one is the door of knowledge, the second one is the door of reason, the third one is the door of patience, and the fourth one is the door of contentment. Know that My Treasure is the heart of a believer.'"

Bihar al-Anwar, vol. 81, "Book of as-Salat," chapter 16, Hadith 59, p. 260
Prophet Muhammad said, "No part of the Salat is yours except that part which you perform with an attentive heart."

Other Shi'a Hadith

Ithaf al-Sadat al-Muttaqin, vol. VII, p. 234
Hadith-e-Qudsi said, "Neither [the vastness of] My earth, nor [that of] My heaven can contain Me. Indeed, it is the heart of the man of faith which can contain Me."

Wasa'il ash-Shi'ah, vol. 4, "Book of as-Salat," section on "The Acts of the Salat," chapter 3, Hadith 1
It is narrated that Imams al-Baqir and as-Sadiq said, "Nothing of your Salat is yours, except that which you did with an attentive heart. So, if one performed it completely mistaken, or neglected its disciplines, it would be folded and thrown back at its owner's face."

Wasa'il ash-Shi'ah, vol. 4, "Book of as-Salat," section on "The Acts of the Salat," chapter 3, Hadith 3

Imam as-Sadiq is quoted to have said, "Eagerness and fear will not get together in a heart unless Paradise is his. So, when you perform your Salat, turn with your heart to God, the Glorified, the Almighty, because there would be no believing servant who would turn with his heart to God, the Exalted, during the Salat and invocation, unless God would turn to him the hearts of the believers, and with their love He would back him and lead him to Paradise."

Sermons, Letters, and Sayings of Imam Ali ibn Abi Talib
(Nahjul Balagha)

"I am amazed at the heart of man: it possesses the substance of wisdom as well as the opposites contrary to it ... for if hope arises in it, it is brought low by covetousness; and if covetousness is aroused in it, greed destroys it."

"'There are four things that make the heart die: wrong action followed by wrong action, playing around with foolish people, spending a lot of time with women, and sitting with the dead.' Then they asked Imam Ali: 'And who are the dead, O Commander of the believers?' He replied: 'Every slave who follows his desires.'"

"Surely want is a trial, and having sickness of the body is more difficult to bear than indigence, and having a sickness of the heart is more difficult to bear than having a sickness of the body. Surely, being very wealthy is a blessing, and having a healthy body is better than being very wealthy, and having awe of God in your heart is better than having a healthy body."

"Surely hearts have desires, and they turn towards, and they turn away ... so approach them by means of what they desire and what they turn towards, for surely if the heart is forced to do some thing against its will, it goes blind."

"Hearts of people are like wild beasts. They attach themselves to those who love and train them."

"Hearts have the tendency of likes and dislikes and are liable to be energetic and lethargic, therefore, make them work when they are energetic because if hearts are forced (to do a thing), they will be blinded."

Imam Ali was asked by one of his companions, Tha'lab al-Yamani, whether he had seen his Lord. Imam Ali replied, "How can I worship something that I do not see?" When asked how he saw Him, Imam Ali replied, "Eyes do not reach Him with physical sight, but the hearts reach Him with the realities of belief."

The Commander of the Faithful, Imam Ali, said, "Everyone who lacks self restraint and piety will have a dead heart; whoever has a dead heart will enter inside the Hell."

"Resignation to the will of God is the cure of the disease of the heart."

"The word of God is the medicine of the heart."

"The disease of the heart is worse than the disease of the body."

"The tongue of a wise man lies behind his heart."

"He who purifies his heart from doubt is a believer."

"What the eye sees the heart preserves."

"The vision of the eye is limited; the vision of the heart transcends all barriers of time and space."

"Enlighten the heart with prayers."

"Strengthen your heart with faith."

"If you love God, tear out your heart's love of the world."

"A hypocrite's tongue is clean, but there is sickness in his heart."

Appendix D

SELECTED SUNNI HADITHS ON THE HEART

Kutub al-Sittah (Six Books)

Sahih Bukhari, vol. 1, book 2, chapter 33, Hadith 44
The Prophet said, "Whoever said *La ilaha illallah* (none has the right to be worshipped but God) and has in his heart good (faith) equal to the weight of a barley grain, will be taken out of Hell. And whoever said: *La ilaha illallah* and has in his heart good (faith) equal to the weight of a wheat grain will be taken out of Hell. And whoever said *La ilaha illallah* (none has the right to be worshiped but God) and has in his heart good (faith) equal to the weight of an atom (or a small ant) will be taken out of Hell."

Sahih Bukhari, vol. 1, book 2, chapter 39, Hadith 52
Prophet Muhammad said, "Beware! There is a piece of flesh in the body, if it becomes good (reformed), the whole body becomes good, but if it gets spoilt, the whole body get spoilt, and that is the heart."

Sahih Bukhari, vol. 1, book 10, chapter 36, Hadith 660

The Prophet said, "God would give shade to seven, on the Day when there will be no shade but His: (These seven persons are:) (1) a just ruler, (2) a youth who has been brought up in the worship of God (i.e. worships God alone sincerely from his childhood), (3) a man whose heart is attached to the mosques [i.e. who offers the five compulsory congregational Salat (prayers) in the mosques], (4) two persons who love each other only for God's sake and they meet and part in God's Cause only, (5) a man who refuses the call of a charming woman of noble birth for illegal sexual intercourse with her and says: I am afraid of God, (6) a man who gives charitable gifts so secretly that his left hand does not know what his right hand has given (i.e. nobody knows how much he has given in charity), and (7) a person who remembers God in seclusion and his eyes become flooded with tears."

Sahih Bukhari, vol. 2, book 19, chapter 16, Hadith 1147

Aishah further said, "I said, 'O God's Messenger! Do you sleep before offering the *Witr* prayers?' He replied, 'O Aishah! My eyes sleep but my heart remains awake!'"

Sahih Bukhari, vol. 6, book 65, chapter 1, Hadith 4937

The Prophet said, "Such a person as recites the Qur'an and masters it by heart, will be with the (angels) honorable and obedient (in heaven). And such a person as exerts himself to learn the Qur'an by heart, and recites it with great difficulty, will have a double reward."

Sahih Bukhari, vol. 8, book 80, chapter 46, Hadith 6377

The Prophet used to say, "O God! Cleanse my heart with the water of snow and hail, and cleanse my heart from all sins as a white garment is cleansed from filth, and let there be a far away distance between me and my sins as You made the east and west far away from each other."

Sahih Bukhari, vol. 9, book 92, chapter 13, Hadith 7086

The Prophet told us that Al-Amanah (the trust or moral responsibility or honesty, and all the duties which God has ordained) descended in the roots of men's hearts (from God) and then they learned it from the

Qur'an and then they learned it from the Prophet's Sunna. The Prophet further told us how that Al-Amanah would be taken away. He said: "Man will go to sleep during which Al-Amanah will be taken away from his heart and only its trace will remain in his heart like the trace of a dark spot; then man will go to sleep, during which Al-Amanah will decrease still further, so that its trace will resemble the trace of blister as when an ember is dropped on one's foot which would make it swell, and one would see it swollen but there would be nothing inside. People would be carrying out their trade but hardly will there be a trustworthy person. It will be said, 'In such and such tribe there is an honest man,' and later it will be said about a man, 'What a wise, polite and strong man he is!' Though he will not have faith equal even to a mustard seed in his heart."

Sahih Bukhari, vol. 9, book 96, chapter 26, Hadith 7364
God's Messenger said, "Recite (and study) the Qur'an as long as your hearts are in agreement as to its interpretation and meanings, but when you have differences regarding its interpretation and meanings, then you should stop reciting it (for the time being)."

Sahih Bukhari, vol. 9, book 97, chapter 35, Hadith 7498
The Prophet said, "God said, 'I have prepared for My righteous slaves (such excellent things) as no eye has ever seen, nor an ear has ever heard nor a human heart can ever think of.'"

Sahih Muslim, vol. 1, book 1, chapter 20, Hadith 179
The Prophet said, "There is no Prophet whom God sent to any nation before me, but he had disciples and companions among his nation who followed his path and obeyed his commands. Then after them came generations who said what they did not do, and did what they were not commanded to do. Whoever strives against them with his hand is a believer; whoever strives against them with his tongue is a believer; whoever strives against them with his heart is a believer. Beyond that there is not even a mustard-seed's worth of faith."

Sahih Muslim, vol. 1, book 1, chapter 39, Hadith 265

The Prophet said, "No one who has an atom's weight of pride in his heart will enter Paradise," A man said, "What if a man likes his clothes to look good and his shoes to look good?" He said, "God is Beautiful and loves beauty. Pride means rejecting the truth and looking down on people."

Sahih Muslim, vol. 1, book 1, chapter 64, Hadith 369
Abu Hudhaifah said, "I heard the Messenger of God say: 'Tribulations will stick to people's hearts like the fibers of a reed mat, one by one. Any heart that imbibes them will get a black spot, and any heart that rejects them will get a white spot, until there will be two types of hearts. One will be white like a smooth stone, which will not be harmed by any tribulation so long as heaven and earth endure. And the other will be black and gloomy, like an overturned vessel, not acknowledging any goodness nor rejecting any evil, except what suits its own whims and desires.'"

Sahih Muslim, vol. 2, book 6, chapter 49, Hadith 1908
There are people who recite the Qur'an and it does not go any deeper than their collarbones, but if it settles in the heart and takes root, it will be beneficial.

Sahih Muslim, vol. 2, book 11, chapter 6, Hadith 2137
The Messenger of God said, "Have you not heard? God does not punish for the tears of the eye or the grief of the heart, rather He punishes for this"—and he pointed to his tongue—"or shows mercy (because of it)."

Sahih Muslim, vol. 3, book 12, chapter 40, Hadith 2420
The Messenger of God said: "Richness is not abundance of (worldly) goods, rather richness is richness of the heart."

Sahih Muslim, vol. 4, book 22, chapter 20, Hadith 4094
Prophet Muhammad said, "In the body there is a piece of flesh. If it is healthy, the entire body will be healthy. But if it is corrupt, the entire body will be corrupt. Verily it is the heart."

Sahih Muslim, vol. 6, book 45, chapter 10, Hadith 6543
The Messenger of God said, "God does not look at your (outward) forms and your wealth, rather He looks at your hearts and your deeds."

Sahih Muslim, vol. 7, book 46, chapter 3, Hadith 6750
Abdullah bin Amr bin Al-As said that he heard the Messenger of God say, "The hearts of the sons of Adam are all between two Fingers of the Most Merciful, like one heart, and He directs them as He wills." Then the Messenger of God said: "O God, controller of the hearts, direct our hearts to obey You."

Sunan Abu Dawood, vol. 2, book 8, chapter 25, Hadith 1510
The Prophet would supplicate: "O Lord! Accept my repentance, and cleanse my sins, and respond to my supplication, and make firm my evidence, and guide my heart, and correct my tongue, and remove the evils (hatred and anger) of my heart."

Jami' At-Tirmidhi, vol. 4, book 34, chapter 61, Hadith 2411
The Messenger of God said, "Do not talk too much without remembrance of God. Indeed excessive talking without remembrance of God hardens the heart. And indeed the furthest of people from God is the harsh-hearted."

Jami' At-Tirmidhi, vol. 6, book 44, chapter 83, Hadith 3334
The Messenger of God said, "Verily, when the slave (of God) commits a sin, a black spot appears on his heart. When he refrains from it, seeks forgiveness and repents, his heart is polished clean. But if he returns, it increases until it cover his entire heart."

Sunan Ibn Majah, vol. 5, book 36, chapter 14, Hadith 3984
The Prophet said, "Beware! In the body there is a piece of flesh that, if it is sound, the whole body will be sound, and if it is corrupt, the whole body will be corrupt. It is the heart."

Sunan Ibn Majah, vol. 5, book 37, chapter 9, Hadith 4143

The Prophet said, "God does not look at your forms or your wealth, rather He looks at your deeds and your hearts."

Sunan Ibn Majah, vol. 5, book 37, chapter 24, Hadith 4216
It was said to the Messenger of God, "Which of the people is best?" He said, "Everyone who is pure of heart and sincere of speech." They said, "Sincere of speech, we know what this is, but what is pure of heart?" He said, "It is (the heart) that is pious and pure, with no sin, injustice, rancor or envy in it."

Sunan An-Nasa'i, vol. 1, book 5, chapter 2, Hadith 453
Two angels came to the Messenger of God and took him to Zamzam, where they split open his stomach and took out his innards in a basin of gold, and washed them with Zamzam water; then they filled his heart with wisdom and knowledge.

Source: Darussalam Global Leader in Islamic Books, Publishers and Distributors, Riyadh, Saudi Arabia.

Al-Musnad Ahmad bin Hanbal

Abu Sa'eed reported: The Messenger of God, peace and blessings be upon him, said, "The hearts are four kinds: a polished heart as shiny as a radiant lamp, a sealed heart with a knot tied around it, a heart that is turned upside down, and a heart that is wrapped. As for the polished heart, it is the heart of the believer and its lamp is the light of faith. The sealed heart is the heart of the unbeliever. The heart that is turned upside down is the heart of a pure hypocrite, for he had knowledge but denied it. As for the heart that is wrapped, it is the heart that contains both faith and hypocrisy. The parable of faith in this heart is the parable of the herb that is sustained by pure water, and the parable of the hypocrisy in it is the parable of an ulcer that thrives upon puss and blood; whichever of the two is greater will dominate."

Abu Thaalaba said: The Messenger of God said, "Righteousness is what achieves tranquility to one's soul and peace to one's heart, while sin disturbs the soul and the heart, even though numerous people should license you (to do it)."

The Messenger of God said, "O God, I seek refuge in Thee from four things: from knowledge that is of no benefit, a heart which is not submissive, a soul which has an insatiable appetite, and a supplication which is not heard."

The Prophet of God said, "When the believer commits sin, a black spot appears on his heart. If he repents and gives up that sin and seeks forgiveness, his heart will be polished. But if (the sin) increases, (the black spot) increases."

Source: Ahmad and Hamza Ahmad al-Zayn Shakir. *Al-Musnad Ahmad bin Hanbal*. 20 vols. Cairo: Dar-al-Hadith, 1995.

References

Abi Talib, Imam Ali ibn. *Nahjul Balagha*. Translated by Farouk Ebeid. Beirut, Lebanon: Dar al-Kitab Al-Lubnani, 1989.

Al-Ashqar, Umar S. *The World of the Jinn and Devils*. Riyadh, Saudi Arabia: International Islamic Publishing House, Second Edition, 2005.

Al-Hanbali, Ibn Rajab, Imam Abu Hamid Al-Ghazali, and Imam Ibn Al-Qayyim. *The Purification of the Soul*. London: Al Firdous Ltd; 3rd edition, May 10, 2015.

Al-Jawziyyah, Ibn Qayyim. *Ighaathat al-Lahfaan*. Translated by Abu Aaliyah Abdullah ibn Dwight Lamont Battle. http//abuaaliyah90.blog. com, November 20, 2012.

Al-Jawziyyah, Ibn Qayyim. *The Sayings of Ibn Qayyim al-Jawziyyah*. Translated by Ikram Hawramani. Independently published, March 25, 2017.

Al-Kulayni, Muhammad ibn Ya'qub. "The Book about People with Divine Authority." In *Kitab Al-Kafi*. Translated by Muhammad Sarwar. New York: Islamic Seminary Inc., August 15, 1999.

Al-Qazwini, Imam Muhammad bin Yazeed ibn Majah. *Sunan Ibn Majah*. Translated by Nasriuddin al-Khattab. Riyadh: Darussalam, 2007.

Al-Qazwini, Sayed Moustafa. *From Resolution to Revolution: The Message of Ashura*. Costa Mesa, California: Islamic Educational Center of Orange County, 2011.

Al-Tirmidhi, Hafiz Abu Elsa. *Jami al-Tirmidhi*. Translation by Abu Khalil. Dar-us-Salam, 2007.

Ali, Abdullah Yusuf. *The Holy Qur'an: Text, Translation and Commentary*. Washington, DC: The Islamic Center, 1978.

Ali, S. V. Mir Ahmed. *The Holy Qur'an: Text, Translation and Commentary*. Elmhurst, New York: Tahrike Tarsile Qur'an Inc., 1995.

American Heart Association. *Heart Disease and Stroke Statistics 2017 At-a-Glance*. https://www.heart.org/idc/groups/ahamah-public/@wcm/@sop/@smd/documents/downloadable/ucm_491265.pdf, 2017.

Baianonie, Imam Mohamed. *Priority of the Deeds of the Heart to the Deeds of the Limbs*. North Carolina: Islamic Center of Raleigh, October 31, 1997.

Bar-On, Reuven. *The Era of the EQ: Defining and Assessing Emotional Intelligence*. Toronto: Paper presented at the 104th Annual Convention of the American Psychological Association, 1996.

Batool, Mehak, Sadia Niazi, and Saba Ghayas. "Emotional Intelligence as a Predictor of Sense of Humor and Hope Among Adults." *Journal of the Indian Academy of Applied Psychology* 40, no. 2 (July 2014): 270–278.

Bechara, Antoine, and Nasir Naqvi. "Listening to Your Heart: Interoceptive Awareness as a Gateway to Feeling." *Nature Neuroscience* 7 (2004): 102–103.

Brace, Robin A. *Yes, the Heart Really Can "Think" and Have Emotions!* http://www.ukapologetics.net/biblicalheart.htm, 2006.

Bronte, Emily. *Wuthering Heights (Wordsworth Classics)*. Wordsworth Editions Ltd. August 5, 1997.

Bryce, Carmen. *Making Choices with Head and Heart*. My Mind: Centre for Mental Wellbeing. May 15, 2017.

CDC. *State Specific Mortality from Sudden Cardiac Death: United States, 1999*. MMWR 51, 6 (2002):123–126.

CDC, NCHS. Underlying Cause of Death 1999-2013 on *CDC WONDER Online Database*, released 2015. Data are from the Multiple Cause of Death Files, 1999–2013, as compiled from data provided by the 57 vital statistics jurisdictions through the Vital Statistics Cooperative Program. Accessed February 3, 2015.

Childre, Sara. *Let Your Heart Talk to Your Brain*. HeartMath Institute, January 20, 2013.

Clarke, E. *Aristotelian Concepts of the Form and Functions of the Brain*. Bull Hist Med 37 (1963): 1–14.

Connor, Steve. *Studies Find Heart Can Affect How We Feel Fear*. Independent, April 7, 2013.

Covey, Stephen R. *The 8ᵗʰ Habit: From Effectiveness to Greatness*. Miniature Edition. New York: Free Press, Simon & Shuster, Inc., 2006.

Daily Mail. *Follow Your Heart and Not Your Head to Make Right Decisions*. http://www.dailymail.co.uk/news/article-413348/Follow-heart-head-make-right-decisions.html, October 29, 2006.

DeLaune, S. C., and P. K. Ladner. *Fundamentals of Nursing: Standards and Practice*, 3ʳᵈ edition. Clifton Park, NY: Thomson Delmar Learning, 2006.

Deutschendorf, Harvey. "Why Emotionally Intelligent People Are More Successful." *Fast Company* magazine, June 22, 2015.

DuBray, W., ed. *Spirituality and Healing: A Multicultural Perspective.* New York: Writers Club Press, 2001.

Ebersole, P., and P. Hess. *Toward Healthy Aging: Human Needs and Nursing Response,* 5th edition. St. Louis, MO: Mosby-Year Book, 1997.

Eckhardt, Lee. *Blue Sky Science: How Does the Brain Get the Heart to Constantly Beat?* Morgridge Institute for Research, https://morgridge. org/blue-sky/how-does-the-brain-get-the-heart-to-constantly-beat/.

El-Naggar, Dr. Zaghloul. *The Human Heart in the Glorious Quran.* The Qur'an Project. Committee on Scientific Notions in the Noble Qur'an, Supreme Council on Islamic Affairs, Cairo, Egypt. http://quranproject. org/The-human-heart-in-the-glorious-Quran-481-d.

Fetterman, Adam K., and Michael D. Robinson. "Do You Use Your Head or Follow Your Heart? Self-Location Predicts Personality, Emotion, Decision Making, and Performance." *Journal of Personality and Social Psychology* 105, no. 2 (Aug 2013): 316–334.

Fontaine, K. L. *Healing Practices: Alternative Therapies for Nursing.* Upper Saddle River: NJ: Prentice Hall, 2000.

Foster, Richard. *Solitude.* IFGATHERING.COM, February 28, 2017.

Frampton, Michael. *Embodiments of Will: Anatomical and Physiological Theories of Voluntary Animal Motion from Greek Antiquity to the Latin Middle Ages, 400 B.C.–A.D. 1300.* Verlag: VDM Verlag Dr. Muller Aktiengesellschaft & Co. KG, Germany, 2008.

Franklin, Benjamin. *Poor Richard's Almanac.* Amazon Digital Services LLC, 2010.

Friday Sermon. *Thinking with the Heart!* http://submission.org/friday_thinking_with_the_heart.html, 2013.

Fullerton, B. "Designing for Solitude." *Interactions* 17, no. 6 (2010): 6–9.

Ghilan, Mohamed. *Intelligence: Is It in the Brain or the Heart.* http://mohamedghilan.com/2012/02/10/intelligence-is-it-in-the-brain-or-the-heart/), February 10, 2012.

Goleman, Daniel. *Emotional Intelligence: Why It Can Matter More Than IQ.* New York: Bantam Books, 1995.

Goleman, Daniel. *Emotional Intelligence: Why It Can Matter More Than IQ.* New York: Bantam Books, 2005.

Gruner, O. C. *Avicenna: The Canon of Medicine.* London: Luzac and Co., 1930.

Gu, J, CB Zhong, and E. Page-Gould. "Listen to Your Heart: When False Somatic Feedback Shapes Moral Behavior." *Journal of Experimental Psychology,* 2012.

Heart Doctor's World. *Is the Heart Organ Responsible for Feelings and Emotions?* https://heartdoctorsworld.wordpress.com/2009/05/20/is-the-heart-organ-responsible-for-feelings-and-emotions/.

Heer, Nicholas. *A Sufi Psychological Treatise.* (*Bayan al-Farq bayn al-Sadr wa-al-Qalb wa-al-Fu'ad wa-al-Lubb* [*The Explanation of the Difference Between the Breast, the Heart, the Inner Heart and the Intellect*]) of Abu 'Abd Allah Muhammad ibn 'Ali al-Hakim al-Tirmidhi, Third Century after the Hijrah, *Muslim World* 5 (January 1961).

Hoffman, Dr. Matthew. *Picture of the Heart.* WebMD, LLC. http://www.webmd.com/heart/picture-of-the-heart#1, 2014.

Ibn Abi Talib, Imam Ali. *Nahjul Balagha (Peak of Eloquence): Sermons and Letters of Imam Ali Ibn Abi Talib.* 12th ed. Islamic Seminary Publications, 1999.

Jarrett, Dr. Christian Jarrett. "Are You A Head Person Or A Heart Person?" *British Psychological Society's* Research Digest *blog,* Science of Us, http://nymag.com/scienceofus/2015/07/are-you-head-person-or-heart-person.html, July 26, 2015.

Jeffrey, D. L. *A Dictionary of Biblical Tradition in English Literature.* Grand Rapids: William B. Eerdmans Publishing, 1992.

Khan, Dr. Muhammad Muhsin. *Sahih Bukhari.* Islamic University, Al-Medina Al-Munauwara. Vols. 1–9, 1994.

Kumar, Gian. *Think from the Heart, Love from the Mind.* CreateSpace Independent Publishing Platform, 2013.

Majlisi, Mohammad Baqir. *Bihar al-Anwar (Ocean of Lights).* Beirut: Dar Ihya al-Turath al Arabi Publications, 1983.

Matthews, D. A., and C. Clark. *The Faith Factor: Proof of the Healing Power of Prayer.* New York: Penguin Books, 1998.

McCraty, R. "Influence of Cardiac Afferent Input on Heart-Brain Synchronization and Cognitive Performance." *International Journal of Psychophysiology* 45, no. 1–2 (2002): 72–73.

McCraty, R. *The Resonant Heart.* Shift: At the Frontiers of Consciousness, December 2004–December 2005, 15–19.

McCraty, Rollin, Raymond Trevor Bradley, and Dana Tomasino. *The Resonant Heart, Shift: At the Frontiers of Consciousness,* 2004.

McCraty, Rollin. *Science of the Heart–Exploring the Role of the Heart in Human Performance.* HeartMath Institute, November 2015.

Micozzi, M. S. *Fundamentals of Complementary and Integrative Medicine*, 3rd edition. St. Louis, MO: Saunders Elsevier, 2006.

Misra, Sidi Abdullah Anik. *Doubts About Islam: I Don't Find Any Observable Effect or Peace in My Worship*. SeekersHub. http://seekershub. org/ans-blog/2010/03/09/doubts-about-islam-i-dont-find-any-observable-effect-or-peace-in-my-worship/, March 9, 2010.

Misra, Sidi Abdullah Anik. *What is the Difference Between the "Heart" (Qalb), "Kindling Heart" (Fuaad), and the "Pure Intellect (Lubb)?* SeekersHub. http://seekershub.org/ans-blog/2009/11/04/what-is-the-difference-between-the-heart-qalb-kindling-heart-fuaad-and-the-pure-intellect-lubb/, November 4, 2009.

Montgomery, Pam. Head and Heart Work Together for Health and Harmony. http://innerself.com/content/living/health/diseases-and-conditions/6055-head-heart-work-together-for-health.html, 2008.

Murphy, D. A., G. W. Thompson, et al. "The Heart Reinnervates After Transplantation." *Annals of Thoracic Surgery* 69, no. 6 (2000): 1769–1781.

Muslim, Imam Abul-Husain. *Sahih Muslim (7 Vol. Set)*. Translated by Nasiruddin al-Khattab. Riyadh: Dar-us-Salam Publications, Inc., 2007.

Olatoye, Raji Mubin. "Towards Understanding the Islamic Concept of the Heart and Its Relationship with Man's Intention/Actions." *European Scientific Journal* (June 2013): 183–189.

Rosenfeld, S. A. *Conversations Between Heart and Brain*. Rockville, MD: National Institute of Mental Health, 1977.

Salovey, Peter, Marc Brackett, and John Mayer. *Emotional Intelligence: Key Readings on the Mayer and Salovey*. Port Chester, New York: Dude Publishing, 2004.

Saucy, Robert. *Minding the Heart: The Way of Spiritual Transformation.* Grand Rapids, Michigan: Kregel Publications, 2013.

Shafi, Shaikh Abu Rumaysah Refi. *Three Types of Hearts.* Islam21C.com, https://www.islam21c.com/spirituality/3333-three-types-of-hearts/, December 9, 2011.

Shakir, Ahmad, and Hamza Ahmad al-Zayn. *Al-Musnad Ahmad bin Hanbal.* Cairo: Dar-al-Hadith, 1995.

Shea, J. *Spirituality and Health Care.* Chicago: Park Ridge Center for the Study of Health, Faith, and Ethics, 2000.

Shirazi, Ayatullah Sayyid Abdul Husayn Dastghaib. *Qalbe Saleem Immaculate Conscience.* CreateSpace Independent Publishing Platform, 2015.

Sinkewicz, Robert E. *Evagrius of Pontus: The Greek Ascetic Corpus.* Oxford Early Christian Studies. New York: Oxford University Press, 2006.

Snyder, C. R. "Hope Theory: Rainbows in the Mind." *Psychological Inquiry,* no. 13 (2002): 249–275.

Solahudin, Dindin. *The Workshop for Morality: The Islamic Creativity of Pesantren Daarut Tauhid in Bandung, Java.* Australia: ANU E Press, the Australian National University, 2008.

Sorajjakool, S., and H. Lamberton, eds. *Spirituality, Health, and Wholeness: An Introductory Guide for Health Care Professionals.* Binghamton, NY: Haworth Press, 2004.

Stacey, Aisha. *Honesty: The Religion of Islam.* IslamReligion.com. https://www.islamreligion.com/articles/1669/honesty/. August 24, 2008.

Surel, Dr. Dominique. *Thinking from the Heart–Heart Brain Science.* Noetic Systems International, January 7, 2015.

Syed, Dr. Ibrahim B. *Humility.* Louisville, Kentucky: Islamic Research Foundation International, Inc. http://WWW.IRFI.ORG.

Tenik, Ali, Dr. Harran U. Ilahiyat Fakultesi, Vahit Goktas, and Dr. Ankara U. Ilahiyat Fakultesi. "Importance and Effects of Remembrance (Dhikr) in Socio-Psychological Terms." *AUIFD* 49 (2008): 217–236.

Thoreau, Henry David. *Walden.* Empire Books, 2013.

Topbas, Osman Nuri. "Tawadhu' (Humility)." https://en.osmannuri topbas.com/tawadhu-humility.html, September 2009.

Turfe, Tallal Alie. *Children of Abraham: United We Prevail, Divided We Fail.* Bloomington, Indiana: iUniverse, 2013.

Turfe, Tallal Alie. *Energy in Islam: A Scientific Approach to Preserving Our Health and the Environment.* Elmhurst, New York: Tahrike Tarsile Qur'an Inc., 2010.

Turfe, Tallal Alie. *Know and Follow the Straight Path: Finding Common Ground between Sunnis and Shi'as.* Bloomington, Indiana: iUniverse, 2015.

Turfe, Tallal Alie. *Patience in Islam: Sabr.* Elmhurst, New York: Tahrike Tarsile Qur'an Inc., 1996.

Turfe, Tallal Alie. *Remember Me, and I Will Remember You (Dhikr: The Soul of Islam).* Bloomington, Indiana, iUniverse, 2016.

Turfe, Tallal Alie. *Unity in Islam: Reflections and Insights.* Elmhurst, New York: Tahrike Tarsile Qur'an Inc., 2004.

Vernon, P. A., R. A. Martin, J. A. Schermer, and A. Mackie. "A Behavioral Genetic Investigation of Humour Styles and Their Correlations with the Big-5 Personality Dimensions." *Personality and Individual Differences* 44 (2008): 1116–1125.

Wallace, Kelly. *Teens Spend a "Mind-Boggling" 9 Hours a Day Using Media.* November 3, 2015, www.cnn.com/2015/11/03/health/teens-tweens-media-screen-use-report.

Walton, Chris. *Does Your Heart Know Your Future? Check This Mind Boggling Research!* Gamma Mindset, www.gammamindset.com, January 24, 2015.

Webb, L. *Conquering the Seven Deadly Sins.* New York: Abingdon Press, 1965.

Za'l, Hafiz Abu Tahir Zubair 'Ali. *Sunan Abu Dawud.* Vols. 1–5. Riyadh: Darussalam, 2008.

Za'l, Hafiz Abu Tahir Zubair 'Ali. *Sunan An-Nasa'i.* Vols. 1–5. Riyadh: Darussalam, 2008.

Index

G

Galinsky, Adam, 21
Gallup Poll, 51
ghusl tartibi (sequence bath), 123
ghusl irtimasi (immersion bath), 123
gluttony, 112
God, belief in, 50–51
Goleman, Daniel, 2, 15–16
gratitude *(shukr)*, 46, 54

H

hadiths, 139–151
hajj (pilgrimage), 117
Halberstadt, Jamin, 29
haq al-yaqin (truth), 104
Hassan (grandson of Muhammad), 6
hatred, 95–97
health
    spirituality and, 88–91
Heart Facts, 16
heart (physical)
    automaticity of, xxiii
    body metaphors and, 23–24
    brain and, xxi, xxii, 10–11, 13–14,
        17–19
    communication of, xx, 13–14
    decision-making and, 20, 22–23,
        26–30
    described, xx, xxii–xxiii
    emotional intelligence and, xx,
        10–11, 17–19
    emotions and, 10–11, 28–29
    functions of, 14–16
    heart brain, 13–14
    heart disease, xxii
    identification with, 21
    intelligence of, xx, xxi, 12–15,
        17–19, 20–24, 26–28
    intrinsic heart rate, xxiii
    intrinsic nervous system, 13–14
    memory transference, 22

heart brain, 13–14
HeartMath Institute, 11, 13–14
honesty *(saraha)*, 52, 58–59
hope, 40–42
Hudhayfah, ibn al-Yaman, 80–81
humility *(tawadhu')*, 52, 56–58, 73–74
humor, 42

I

Ibn al-Jawzi, Abu'l-Faraj, xv
Ibn Qayyim, Al-Jawziyyah, 81
Ibn Sina, 17
idrak an-nafs (self-realization), 118–121
ignorance, 96-97
ihsan (perfection), 121
ikhlas (devotion), 52, 54–55, 105
imam (leader), 79
Imam Ali, 53, 79-80
Imam Hassan, 6
Imam Hussein, 6
immersion, 122–124
inner heart *(fuaad)*, 82–83, 85
infaq (generosity), 54, 105
intellect, xxi,1, 11, 17-19, 82-85, 126
intelligence, types of, 17–19
intelligence quotient (IQ), 15–16, 18
intelligence testimonials, 20
intention *(niyyah)*, 70–71, 123, 126
interpersonal v. intrapersonal skills, 3
intrinsic cardiac adrenergic cells, 14
intuition, 29
inverted heart *(qalb al-mankus)*, 73
Islam
    dhikr and, 52–53
    emotional intelligence and, 11
    Sunni and Shi'a conflict, 34, 36
Islamic personality
    development of, 65–66, 116–118
    immersion and, 122–124
    revolving hierarchy of, 118–122